FIRES ON THE MOUNTAIN

THE MACEDONIAN REVOLUTIONARY MOVEMENT
AND THE KIDNAPPING OF ELLEN STONE

by

LAURA BETH SHERMAN

EAST EUROPEAN MONOGRAPHS, BOULDER
DISTRIBUTED BY COLUMBIA UNIVERSITY PRESS
NEW YORK

1980

DR701
M4
S44

PHOTO, JACKET COVER: left, Khristo Chernopeev;
right: Yane Sandansky

Copyright ©1980 by Laura Beth Sherman
Library of Congress Card Catalog Number 79-56521
ISBN 0-914710-55-9

Printed in the United States of America

FIRES ON THE MOUNTAIN

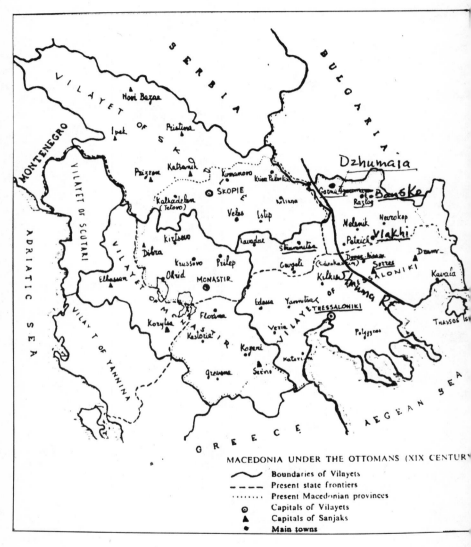

MACEDONIA
Showing the travels of the kidnappers' band
(*Cities and villages mentioned in the story are underlined*)

TABLE OF CONTENTS

LIST OF ILLUSTRATIONS

JACKET COVER:
Xhristo Chernopeev and Yane Sandansky

FRONTISPIECE:
Map of Macedonia, showing travels of the kidnappers' band.

PLATE I.
Sava Mixhailov, Yane Sandansky, Krustio Asenov

PLATE II.
Ellen Stone

PLATE III.
Katerina Tsilka and baby Elena

PLATE IV.
Yane Sandansky's band in late 1902 or early 1903

PLATE V.
Xhristo Chernopeev's band in 1903.

PLATE VI.
Typical Macedonian band, circa 1903.

PLATE VII.
A typical Balkan town of the turn of the century.

PLATE VIII.
A typical Balkan town of the turn of the century.

Introduction

From September, 1901 to February, 1902, the name Ellen Stone appeared in the American press far more frequently than that of any other woman: "American Missionary Kidnapped in Macedonian Turkey!"; "Where is Ellen Stone?"; "Negotiations Drag On—Stone Not Yet Released." Church congregations prayed for her safety; people across the country contributed money for her ransom—including the ambassador to the United States of Her Imperial Majesty, the Empress of China. Members of Congress demanded to know why the Department of State had not yet arranged for Ellen Stone's safe return.

This publicity transformed a fifty-five-year-old, overweight spinster into a heroine. Ellen Stone had been sent to European Turkey by the American Board of Foreign Missions. She was kidnapped and held for $100,000 ransom (equal to at least ten times that sum today) by members of the Internal Revolutionary Organization of Macedonia and Adrianople (IMRO), a group struggling for liberation from Turkish rule. Their leader, Yane Sandansky, became the romantic hero of folksong and story throughout the Balkans and streets and towns in Bulgaria and Yugoslavia bear his name today.

I first learned of the Ellen Stone story while doing graduate work in Bulgaria, at the University of Sofia. A Bulgarian friend lent me IMRO publications of the 1920s. There I saw photographs of Sandansky's band and other Macedonian revolutionaries. Fiercely moustachioed and bearded, draped with chest bandoliers (some of them empty of cartridges), they stare out at us in attitudes of contrived casualness, holding rifles, or swords, or long pistols. My friend also gave me a 180-page biography of Sandansky's sidekick, Khristo Chernopeev, written by Chernopeev's son. It had neither been noticed by Bulgarian historians nor translated by foreign scholars.

With these materials in hand, I decided to write a paper or perhaps an article on the Ellen Stone kidnapping. But I could not explain why Stone was kidnapped without first explaining why there was a Macedonian liberation movement. These considerations led me into the intricacies of Balkan politics between 1876 and 1900. This book is the result.

Introduction

I am indebted to many people for help in these investigations. For research facilities and materials, I would like to acknowledge the assistance of the National Library of Bulgaria "Kiril i Metodii," the University of Sofia "Kliment Okhridski" and its Faculty of History, and most particularly the Institute of History of the Bulgarian Academy of Sciences. I am grateful as well to the Foreign Ministry of the People's Republic of Bulgaria for the use of its diplomatic archives, and to the ministry's staff for their courteous and kind attention. I would like to thank all the members of the American embassy in Sofia for their moral support, especially Dick and Patty Bossard who gave me shelter at a particularly crucial time. Most of all, I am grateful and thankful for the advice, encouragement, patience and editorial abilities of my husband, Harvey J. Feldman.

In transliterating Bulgarian to English, I have used the Library of Congress phonetic system.

Washington, D.C.   L.B.S.
April, 1979

Chapter I
The Founding of IMRO

The revolutionary movement in Macedonia and Adrianople can be understood only as a continuation of the 500-year struggle of the Bulgarian people against the Ottoman Empire. From 1396 when the Ottomans captured Turnovo, the capital of the Second Bulgarian Empire, until the establishment of the Principality of Bulgaria in 1877, Bulgaria did not exist as a state and was unfamiliar as a political entity to most Europeans. Bulgarian language and culture were preserved during the five centuries of Turkish rule in isolated monasteries and mountain villages, which Turkish rulers ignored as long as taxes were regularly paid. The Turks also tolerated a few strategically located Bulgarian towns, giving them local autonomy and exemption from taxes in return for military service. In such towns, the Orthodox religion and Bulgarian language and culture also survived.

During the decline of the Ottoman Empire in the eighteenth and nineteenth centuries, the Bulgarian population suffered terribly from exorbitant taxation and the harassment of roaming armies of disbanded soldiers. Isolated from liberal trends in Europe and cowed by their proximity to Constantinople, the Bulgarians reasserted their traditional heritage more slowly than did the Greeks or Serbs. In 1762, Otetz Paisii, a monk living on Mount Athos, sparked the revival of Bulgarian national consciousness with his book, *A History of the Bulgarian People*, which recounted the glories and triumphs of Bulgarian tsars and saints. With renewed interest in Bulgarian heritage, a cultural renaissance began: histories, grammars, and religious tracts were surreptitiously printed or smuggled across the Danube from Bucharest; in 1850 the first Bulgarian language school opened in Gabrovo.

With the literary revival came a reaction against Greek control of the Orthodox church. In a country where all facets of human life—birth, death, education, local government—were church-supported and operated, Greek spiritual domination had been a major factor in the effacement of Bulgarian culture. Revival of this culture required Bulgarian schools and priests and a Slavonic liturgy—in short, an autonomous Bulgarian church.

Thus, the pioneers of Bulgarian nationalism, Rakovski, Panayotov, and Xadzhi Dimitur, fought first to establish a Bulgarian church. After their forty years of struggle, in 1870, the Sultan agreed to recognize the Bulgarian Exarchate, a Bulgarian church hierarchy conducting services in Church Slavonic. In a special *firman* of 1870, the exarchate was given administrative and spiritual jurisdiction over fifteen dioceses in European Turkey; however, the Greek Patriarchate made it very difficult for the exarchate to exercise its rights in these dioceses.

The fate of the Christian populations in Bulgaria, Bosnia, Serbia, and Herzegovina had been an issue for the Great Powers for a number of years. All pressure applied on the Turks to grant civil and church reforms to these Christians had gone unheeded. In response to the massacre of Bulgarian Christians after the April Uprising in 1876, the Great Powers assembled at Constantinople to discuss once again Turkish intransigence.[1]

Russia was convinced that only complete autonomy would provide sufficient protection for the Christians in the Balkans, but the other powers, particularly Austria-Hungary and England, refused to allow the dismantling of the Ottoman Empire. Since Austria would not discuss the autonomy of Bosnia and Herzegovina, the only question before the conference was the organization of a Bulgarian province. Russia suggested an autonomous province of Bulgaria stretching from Bourgas on the Black Sea to Dedeagatch on the Aegean, from Lake Okhrid to Nish and Vidin, to be ruled by a governor-general, appointed by the Sultan, and by a provincial assembly, elected locally. The province would be organized under the supervision of foreign troops temporarily occupying it.

Austria and England strongly objected to Russia's proposal, each for different reasons. Austria feared that so large a Bulgarian province would give Russia dominance in the eastern half of the Balkans and attract to her such other Slav provinces as Bosnia and Herzegovina, which Austria considered her domain. England saw a large Bulgaria as fatal to the independence of the Ottoman Empire because the Slav element would hold a most strategic position in and a large part of the resources of the empire, thus reducing it to a minor power.

Countering the Russian plan, Lord Salisbury suggested dividing the proposed area into two parts, one with a capital at Sofia, the other at Turnovo. Each part would be governed by a governor-general, nominated by the Porte with the consent of the Guaranteeing Powers for a five-year term, and assisted by a provincial assembly. The Ottoman army would be concentrated in towns and fortresses, and a

newly created local national militia and gendarmerie would carry out
ordinary police functions. All of these reforms were to be introduced
and supervised by an international commission assisted by European
gendarmerie. The Bulgarians, of course, were delighted with Salisbury's proposals. Russia, although not completely satisfied, acquiesed,
and Austria went along with the plan in order to keep peace with its
neighbors. The Porte rejected outright the plan for two autonomous
Bulgarian provinces, and Russia declared war on the Ottoman Empire.

By 1877, Russia occupied all the northern territories of the Ottoman Empire and threatened Constantinople. Now, instead of accept-
ing a large Bulgaria divided into two parts and ruled by an Ottoman
governor-general, the defeated Turks conceded an autonomous Bulgarian principality. Under the Treaty of San Stefano, a "preliminary
treaty," signed by Turkey and Russia on February 17, 1878, almost
three-quarters of the Balkan peninsula united to form a greater Bulgaria. Stretching from Pirot, Nish, Skopje, Debar, Okhrid, and
Kastoria in the west to the Black Sea as far as Bourgas in the east
(but not including Adrianople), and from just north of Salonika in
the south to the Danube River in the north, this principality realized
all the national aspirations of the Bulgarian people. Comprising
63,975 square kilometers, the Principality of Bulgaria completely
cut off Constantinople from her territory in Bosnia, Herzegovina,
western Greece, and Albania. Although the Bulgaria created by the
Treaty of San Stefano clearly followed the boundaries accepted by
the Great Powers in 1876 at the conference in Constantinople, by
1878, they were no longer willing to accept such a state. Citing treaties of 1858 and 1871, England notified Russia that any modifica-
tions of boundaries in the Ottoman Empire had to be approved by all
signatories of the earlier treaties and therefore, Russia, even though
she had defeated the Ottomans, alone had no power to dictate changes
in the Balkans. Austria concurred, and Russia herself suggested a
conference in Berlin of the Great Powers to reconsider the Treaty of
San Stefano.

In June of 1878, the Powers met to revise the treaty and to realign
the boundaries. The subsequent Treaty of Berlin, signed on July 13,
1878, laid the bases for the revolutionary movement in Macedonia
and Adrianople. It divided the Principality of Bulgaria (created by
the Treaty of San Stefano) into three separate areas: the first, a principality whose borders ended at the Rila Mountains in the south and
Kiustendil and Vidin in the west; the second, the areas of Vratsa,

Pirot, and Nish, which were given to Serbia; and the third, the area between the Rhodopes and the Balkan mountains which became the province of Eastern Roumelia, under the direct political and military authority of the Sultan, but with local administrative autonomy and a Christian governor-general. All other territory was returned to Turkey, which gave vague promises of reforms.

Macedonia and Adrianople were not specifically mentioned in the treaty. They fell under the rubric of "other parts of Turkey in Europe for which no special organization has been provided for by the present treaty."[2] Under Article 23, the Porte committed itself to "apply scrupulously" laws similar to the Organic Law granted Crete originally in 1868.[3] This law was to be adapted to local conditions in each area by a special commission, appointed by the Porte, in which "native elements" were largely represented. A European commission instituted to oversee the establishment of Eastern Roumelia was to approve also all laws adopted for Macedonia and Adrianople.

Applying the Organic Law of Crete to Macedonia and Adrianople was not an easy task. Unlike Crete's, the population was not homogeneous, neither was it easily divided into two distinct nationalities as Crete was divided into Greeks and Turks. There was not one dominant language, or one dominant religion; for example, Macedonia was inhabited by Greeks, Serbs, Albanians, Vlachs, Bulgarians, Gypsies, and Jews. Half-hearted attempts were made to draft a law of reforms for Macedonia, but the Great Powers, reluctant to push Turkey, took no steps to ameliorate the plight of the non-Turkish population in Macedonia and Adrianople. Thus, in these areas, Article 23 remained ineffectual.

Bulgarians everywhere greeted the decisions of the Berlin Congress with great indignation. Petitions, proposals, memorandums, and angry letters from Bulgarians bombarded the European commission meeting in Eastern Roumelia to organize that province, and also the ambassadors of the Great Powers in Constantinople. The population of one small Bulgarian town in Macedonia, Velles, expressed its dismay at the "mortal blow" which the Treaty of Berlin inflicted upon them: they pleaded that all cities with Bulgarian majorities be unified into a *vilayet* (a separate administrative region), such as Crete, with its administrative center at Skopje, in which the reforms granted in the Berlin Treaty could be introduced.[4] Macedonian Bulgarians living in Constantinople proposed even more specific reforms to maintain "peace and order" in Macedonia. In a letter to the Great Power ambassadors, they insisted that all those dioceses in Macedonia which were predominantly Bulgarian and under the authority of the Bulgarian Exarchate be united into a separate vilayet.[5]

The administative reforms demanded for in a "Bulgarian" vilayet in European Turkey would make it all but independent of the Ottoman Empire. The Bulgarians in the vilayet of Bitola wanted reforms in the composition and workings of the courts, in the makeup of the gendarmerie and the police, and in the tax system; they wished to choose members of the administration, judiciary and police, according to the national makeup of the vilayet, and to designate as the official language, in addition to Turkish, the language spoken by the majority of the population of their area.[6]

Because of tight censorship of newspapers published in the Ottoman Empire and the illegality of political activity in Macedonia, the peoples' demands for reform were publicized only in the press of the Bulgarian principality and in *Zornitsa*, a Bulgarian language newspaper published in Constantinople by American missionaries. From continual discussions the idea of an autonomous Macedonian province developed and led to the revival of armed struggle in Macedonia.[7]

Support for the struggle against the Turks in Macedonia came from the Bulgarian principality. In late summer of 1878, Turkish raids on villages near Melnik spurred Bulgarians in the cities along the Bulgarian-Turkish border to organize, arm, and retaliate against the Turks. Under the auspices of a newly created committee, "Unity," former volunteers in the Russo-Bulgarian army in Kiustendil and Gorna Dzhumaia crossed the border into Turkey to protect the Bulgarian population from further Turkish attack.

Between October 5 and 18, 1878, half-a-dozen bands campaigned against the Turks in the area around Krecna. The Kresnensko-Razloshkoto Uprising, as it was called, rapidly spread through the villages in the Struma Valley with little resistance, at first, from the Turks. To mobilize the population, the bands organized local administrative organs in each village they controlled. One such group declared the independent republic of Macedonia.

The Turks proposed talks to settle differences. When the talks failed in early November, the Turks launched counterattacks which slowly crushed the rebellion. By May of 1879 it was all over. A second attempt to overthrow the Turks was planned for 1880 in the area around Bitola and Okhrid, but this, too, failed when the plan was leaked to the Turkish authorities.[8]

In 1879 a secret organization was formed, at the initiative of the ruling party in the principality, to work for the unification of Macedonia, Eastern Roumelia, and the principality. With branches in Sofia and Plovdiv, the organization hoped to use Gladstone's support for a unified Bulgaria—plus a new Russo-Turkish war—to cover their uprising. When it became evident that neither Gladstone nor Russia was willing to go to war for Bulgaria, the organization disbanded.

In the years following the signing of the Berlin treaty, the situation for the Bulgarian population in Macedonia worsened considerably. In addition to a backward economy, exorbitant taxes, and outdated laws, the population suffered raids by roving bandits. Also, determined to prevent the loss of Macedonia to the principality, the Turks erected every possible barrier to the development of a Bulgarian national consciousness among the Macedonians. They denied permission for Bulgarian schools and priests in many areas and instead encouraged Greek and Serbian activities, and refused to implement Article 23 of the Berlin treaty, despite Bulgarian, Russian, and Great Power pressures.

Bulgarians in the principality made sporadic attempts to organize a movement for the liberation of Macedonia. In the beginning, they founded charity organizations to aid Turkish terror victims and refugees from Macedonia, and to gather educational materials for distribution there. Some formed societies to agitate for the abrogation of the Berlin treaty, while others concentrated on forcing Turkey to institute the promised reforms.

In 1885, a serious attempt to liberate Macedonia occurred in conjunction with the unification of Eastern Roumelia and the principality. Dimitür Rizov and Zakhari Stoyanov established a special organization, the Bulgarian Secret Central Revolutionary Committee, to send armed bands into Macedonia. The committee dispatched students from Sofia and Plovdiv to towns and villages to collect money and weapons for armed bands. But these bands never crossed into Macedonia. Under pressure from the Great Powers, the principality withdrew its support from the committee and took strong measures to prevent an uprising in Macedonia in order to assure the Powers' assent to unification of Eastern Roumelia and the principality.

Discontent was widespread in Macedonia. But as in Bulgaria, its expression was disorganized, without central leadership or an articulated goal. While political jockeying had prevented the formation of a united Macedonian movement in Bulgaria, lack of leadership was the problem in Macedonia. The intelligentsia, who had spearheaded the original national revival and had organized the 1876 liberation struggle, fled to the principality to escape Turkish censorship and oppression. It took time and the spread of Bulgarian language schools and churches in Macedonia before a new intelligentsia could develop.

The schools were the centers of the Bulgarian national consciousness and, consequently, of the anti-Turk movement. Schoolteachers and students alike were well-acquainted with the history of the liberation movement in Bulgaria during the 1870s. Their heroes were leaders of that movement: Vasil Levski, Khristo Botev, Ben Rakovski, Zakhari Stoyanov. In a number of Macedonian towns, small, independent groups emerged to study the revolutionary literature of the previous struggle. In 1888-89, Pere Toshev, later to become one of the most active leaders of IMRO, formed such a group among the students at the Bulgarian Boys' High School in Salonika. At the same time, Ivan Xadzhinikolov, a future founder of IMRO, organized the teachers at the same school.

By 1893, these study groups assumed a more formal shape. Damian Gruev, Dr. Khristo Tatarchev, Ivan Xadzhinikolov, Peter Poparcov, Andon Dimitrov and Khristo Bantandzhiev met to discuss a liberation organization for the first time on October 23, 1893. They took no formal action but pledged to spread the idea that armed struggle was essential in order to liberate Macedonia. At the beginning of 1894, the same six men gathered for a second meeting, which formally established the Macedonian Revolutionary Organization (IMRO) and its leading organ, the Central Macedonian Revolutionary Committee.[9] While the statutes and regulations governing the internal workings of the organization have not survived, it is clear from memoirs of participants that IMRO looked to the pre-1878 Bulgarian national revolution as a model for their own struggle.[10] Poparcov, who wrote the original statutes, worked from the statutes of the Fighting Central Bulgarian Committee of 1867.[11]

The impetus for the founding of IMRO was a desire to preserve the ethnicity of the Bulgarian population in Macedonia. "Foreign" propaganda had increased tremendously in Macedonia in the late 1880s and early 1890s, and seemed a very tangible threat to Bulgarian patriots. Serbian propaganda particularly concerned IMRO's original members. Damian Gruev explained that even though Serbian propaganda was not mentioned in IMRO's "Rules and Regulations," the need to "ward off the effects of such propaganda by bringing the people around to our side" was definitely on their minds.[12] Ivan Xadzhinikolov claimed that the creation of a revolutionary organization, such as IMRO, was the only means of neutralizing outside influences. It would be "the most secure base for saving Bulgarian ethnicity and strengthening the population spiritually and economically."[13] Another founder of IMRO, Poparcov, decried the Turks' "brutal policy" of turning the population of Macedonia into Serbs. Such a policy, he contended, "offends the dignity of every Macedonian Bulgarian and cruelly wounds their national feelings." To Poparcov and his comrades, forced adoption of Serbian nationality was a tragedy for the million Bulgarians living in Macedonia. It entailed not only the loss of their own culture, but also the acceptance of the authority of the Greek Patriarchate, against which Bulgarians had waged so long and persistent a struggle.[14]

The founders of IMRO and those who later supported them insisted that the Turkish attitude toward the Bulgarian population, exemplified by official encouragement of Serbian and Greek nationalist propaganda, precluded a successful struggle by peaceful means. Preservation of Bulgarian ethnicity, they were sure, depended on political independence for the population of Macedonia. IMRO did not preach direct union with the principality, because its founders were well aware that international sentiment firmly opposed such a union. Instead, they called for "autonomy for that part of Macedonia inhabited chiefly by Bulgarians." Such autonomy was only a means, first of easing the incorporation of Macedonia with the principality and eventually, of uniting all the Balkan peoples into a federation.[15] After their second meeting in Salonika, the six founding members split up to spread the work in other Macedonian cities. They carried out agitational work without a formal system, but through a network of friends and relatives a loose confederation of Macedonian patriots evolved.

Damian Gruev started the first local branches of IMRO. During the summer of 1894, he travelled through western Macedonia, visiting Shtip, Prilep, Bitola, Resen, Okhrid, and Struma. In each city, he formed small revolutionary groups, or at least converted a few individuals who promised to continue the propaganda work. Gruev's most successful convert during this tour was a schoolteacher he talked to in Shtip, Gotse Delchev. In a short time, Delchev and Gruev managed to organize the majority of Shtip's Bulgarian population into committees and appoint a network of activists to preach in the neighboring countryside.[16]

The revolutionary movement spread rapdily through other areas of Macedonia. Georcho Petrov and Pere Toshev used their teaching jobs in Bitola to cover organization work among the local peasantry. Others propagandized in eastern Macedonia and in Adrianople. The groups these men formed were to promote the idea of Macedonian liberation through the study of Bulgarian revolutionary history and Bulgarian newspapers. But most of the time such literature was scarce, even in big cities. According to IMRO historian Khristo Siliyanov, "members spent their time twiddling their thumbs and fantasizing on the possible ways of avenging the Turks for their five centuries of tyranny."[17] The leaders of the movement lacked any sort of military or political training. In the beginning all they wanted to do was to organize groups throughout Macedonia and "undertake something with 'bombs' against Turkey."[18] Even so, the revolutionary idea spread quickly through the intelligentsia in Macedonia, and by 1896 there was a thin, but widespread network of converts.

The increase in membership provoked a need for a more centralized direction and a specific hierarchy to organize a successful uprising. Local committees needed materials to study, a means of communicating with each other, and training weapons. In 1896, Delchev set up a postal network through which IMRO could send and receive letters and literature. At points along the Turkish-Bulgarian border (Samokov, Kiustendil, Dupnitsa), Delchev staffed crossing stations to aid illegal travel and weapon supplies, but within Macedonia, no particular system existed.

Organizational work depended on the initiative of the local organizer. While Gruev was teaching in Shtip in 1894-95, the central committee in Salonika lay dormant, reviving only upon Gruev's return. In Skopje, the local chairman, Khristo Matev, paid more attention to combating Serbian propaganda than to organizing revolutionary groups. To consolidate IMRO and more clearly define its aims and methods, the most active members met in Salonika in the spring of 1896. In attendance were all six original members plus Gotse Delchev, Georcho Petrov, Khristo Matev, Kiril Perlichev, and Khristo Kotsev. Although the congress was conducted informally, without bureau or chairman, it is regarded by historians as the constituent congress of IMRO, establishing its aims and structure. In 1897, Delchev and Petrov published these as "Statutes" and "Rules and Regulations" of the "Bulgarian Revolutionary Committee of Macedonia and Adrianople."[19]

The revolutionary committee dedicated itself to fight for "full political autonomy for Macedonia and Adrianople." Since they sought autonomy only for those areas inhabited by Bulgarians, they denied other nationalities membership in IMRO. According to Article 3 of the statutes, any Bulgarian could become a member, "regardless of sex, as long as he or she had not compromised themselves with anything dishonorable or anti-social and [was] willing to promise to be useful to the cause of liberation." Once accepted into IMRO, a member was obliged to fight for the "independence of Bulgarians in Macedonia and Adrianople." ("Rules and Regulations," Article 15). The uprising, necessary to win independence, was a vision for the future. In the meantime, IMRO had to awaken the national consciousness of the Bulgarians and convince them that self-defense was the only path to a successful revolution ("Statutes," Article 2).[20]

The illegal organization needed a highly centralized structure to maintain its secrecy and effectiveness. They divided the territory into seven revolutionary regions with centers at Salonika, Bitola, Skopje, Struma, Serres, and Adrianople, with the Salonika committee acknowledged as central. They further subdivided each region into counties, each county into districts, and each district into local committees. The number of committees and the boundaries of their activities were determined by the next higher committee in the area. All messages to and from lower committees had to pass through the applicable regional committee, which alone had the right to communicate directly with the central committee in Salonika through a special code.

On each level a committee was composed of a chairman, a secretary, a treasurer, and a few advisers. Ordinary members of the organization, called "workers," were divided into groups, each with its own leader who answered to the chairman of the next higher committee. Secret internal police kept track of the organization's enemies and potential traitors. Each type of offense committed against IMRO carried a suitable punishment and was enforced by the secret police.

The Salonika Congress of 1896 discussed one other important question, the need to have a permanent representative in Sofia to serve as a link to the outside world, to explain IMRO's aims, and to raise money for its activities. As there were no volunteers for the job at the time of the congress, the question lay idle for a few months. However, at the end of 1896, while teaching in Bansko, Gotse Delchev was forced to flee to Bulgaria because he was suspected by Turkish administrators of revolutionary activity. During the spring of 1897,

Georcho Petrov arrived in Sofia for the same reason. Thus Delchev and Petrov, more by default than by desire, became the representatives of IMRO in Sofia. Delchev involved himself in the more practical aspects of the movement, collecting money, weapons, and revolutionary literature and shipping them to Macedonia, while Petrov maintained ties and negotiated with Macedonian societies, representatives of Bulgarian political parties and the Bulgarian government.

In March 1895, activists for Macedonian liberation in Bulgaria established the Supreme Macedonian Committee.[21] According to the statutes published at the end of its first congress, the supreme committee aimed for the "acquisition of political autonomy, applied and guaranteed by the Great Powers, for the people of Macedonia and Adrianople."[22] The means of galvanizing government and public opinion in Bulgaria and Europe to support the Macedonian movement were to be newspaper articles, agitation and meetings, delegations and memorandums to European capitals; if such action proved ineffective, the committee would turn to "such actions, as the strength of the situation dictated."[23]

One of the first actions of the supreme committee was to organize a large-scale military incursion into Macedonia in the summer of 1895. A number of detachments were formed in Bulgaria, commanded by reserve officers and volunteers from the Bulgarian army. These bands entered Turkey intent on proving to the outside world that Macedonia was ripe for revolution. In this way they hoped to compel Turkey to introduce the promised reforms. The bands did not remain in Turkey for long. After suffering heavy casualties in skirmishes with Turkish troops, they retreated to Bulgaria.[24]

IMRO remained on the sidelines during the supreme committee's incursion into Turkey. Its members neither knew of the plans beforehand nor chose to participate when the bands crossed the border. Petrov reported from Bitola that the action was followed with curiosity and sympathy, but in no way contributed to popularizing the idea of an internal uprising. When Gruev met with the leaders of the supreme committee in Sofia in 1896 to report on the state of the revolutionary movement in Macedonia and ask for help in future work, he told them that the insurrection had disrupted IMRO's plans. But at least, he added, it was comforting to know that the emigrants in Bulgaria were working more seriously for the independence of Macedonia.[25]

Members of IMRO sought material and financial support from the supreme committee in a series of meetings in Sofia in 1895 and 1896. General Danail Nikolaev, the head of the committee, tied financial aid to IMRO's agreement to recognize the supreme committee as the sole representative of the Macedonian movement in Bulgaria and abroad and as the decisive voice in determining when a general uprising should occur.[26] Gruev, Delchev, and Petrov met skepticism everywhere that IMRO would be effective or could lead a serious revolutionary uprising. IMRO was looked upon as an association of naive idealists who had neither strength nor influence in Macedonia. In a meeting with Petrov in 1896, General Nikolaev said that "with the [Macedonian] peasantry, nothing can be accomplished, nothing serious." The only way to liberate Macedonia was to raise an army of 20,000 to 30,000 soldiers in Bulgaria and invade.[27]

Having failed to receive help from the supreme committee, Delchev and Petrov, as IMRO's representatives in Sofia, turned to the Bulgarian government itself. From about 1895 to 1897, the government showed a willingness to help IMRO financially and materially, for its own reasons. Such aid aimed at weakening the supreme committee, over which the government had little control, and at preventing IMRO from acting in a manner harmful to the principality's foreign policy. In a meeting with Petrov in 1896, the Inspector of Police of Sofia offered to divert to IMRO a large sum of money which was being sent to the supreme committee by English well-wishers, but Petrov refused to "steal" their money.

In a gesture of goodwill, in 1896, the government, through its commercial agent in Skopje, Dimitur Risov, offered IMRO 6,000 leva in cash and 20,000 leva worth of weapons. The organization willingly accepted the gifts but refused to agree to the condition that none of the weapons be sent to the province of Adrianople, a request which was considered "undue meddling in Internal Committee affairs."[29] In its turn, the government decided not to hand over the promised cash or to supply ammunition with the rifles, telling the central committee that IMRO would have to pay for the ammunition although the government knew IMRO had no funds. As a result, IMRO distributed the rifles without bullets. The incident convinced the members that the government was more interested in controlling IMRO than in aiding it, and they refused to have any further dealings with the Bulgarian government.

IMRO's stubborn insistence on maintaining its independence prevented it from receiving significant support in the principality. Yet there was really no other source of money or materials on which IMRO could depend. The Macedonian peasantry, to the degree they thought about liberation, agreed with General Nikolaev of the supreme committee: "Whatever they received would come from Bulgaria."[30] Even members of IMRO were of little help. Specific rules for collecting money for the cause had been set forth in IMRO's "Statutes" and "Rules and Regulations" in 1896.[31] But dues were very low and contributions hard to get. From a whole summer's propagandizing, one band received about $1,250 (310 Turkish *lira*); enough to keep them fed and clothed while they travelled and to buy twenty-six rifles.[32]

Money, or, more properly, the lack of it, was a constant source of anxiety for IMRO. According to Petrov, the "pressure from the population for weapons was great. Local leaders everywhere felt the need for material proof of the organization's strength and of the effectiveness of its means and their applicability in the case of an armed struggle."[33] Even the ammunition-less rifles which IMRO had received from the Bulgarian government raised IMRO's reputation. But much more was needed, and thus the central committee came more and more to depend on "forced contributions" and "get-rich-quick" schemes to supplement the treasury.

Robberies, extortions, and kidnappings were all considered as possible expedients. Although many authors have excused such acts as being justified by the revolutionary aim, at least some of IMRO's members doubted the morality of such actions.[34] Delchev, for example, did not consider thievery a proper activity in the Macedonian struggle, but he accepted individual acts as personal sacrifices for the cause. "There can be no boundaries to such sacrifices even though they might destroy your name and honor. . . . If we consider the opinion of the people, we can have peace of mind. . . many are man's measures of morality and immorality."[35] In fact, Delchev was the first to suggest that a member of IMRO use illegal means to obtain money. In 1896, with Delchev's approval, a Kiustendil postal worker and IMRO member stole 20,000 *lira* ($80,000) from the postal cash box. He escaped with the money, but was so hotly pursued that he dropped the sack of money into a river, and it was never recovered.[36]

Many of the schemes proposed were far-fetched. For example, Boris Sarafov suggested first the kidnapping of King Alexander of Serbia as he travelled to Hillendar Monastery on Mount Athos, then his own kidnapping which, because he travelled on a Russian passport, would force the Russian ambassador to pay a ransom. Wilder still was his suggestion to the American consul in St. Petersburg that a detachment of Macedonian volunteers be sent to help the Americans in the Spanish-American War in exchange for American financial support of the Macedonian struggle.[37]

Some fund-raising schemes cost IMRO more in lives and money than it received from them. Turkish authorities avenged almost every kidnapping or robbery, whether by IMRO or by local bandits. Ensuing persecution and mass arrest of Bulgarians living near the scene of the crime often resulted in great losses of materials, members, and sympathizers for IMRO. The first major example of such revenge, the repetition of which IMRO members sought constantly to avoid, was the Vinishka affair. In a witch-hunt through Bulgarian villages after brigands killed a local Turkish landlord and stole 800 *lira* ($200), the Turks discovered a cache of rifles and literature which revealed to them IMRO's existence and its aims. By the time Turkish counteraction ended as a result of pressure exerted by the European embassies in Constantinople, ten Bulgarians had died, 200 had been tortured, 500 had been jailed, 300 had been forced to flee to Bulgaria, and IMRO had lost its most important workers in Shtip and Skopje. In another case, a year later, an IMRO band kidnapped a rich Greek doctor in Lozengrad, but the 800 *lira* ransom they received barely covered assistance to those arrested or tortured in retaliation.

The helplessness with which IMRO watched such atrocities stemmed from its lack of permanent armed and trained bands in the countryside which could organize local resistance and protect village and organizational interests. Delchev, for example, on hearing about the Vinishka affair, went to Bulgaria to organize a large band to "attack the overflowing jails of Shtip and Skopje."[38] He also asked Boris Sarafov to collect, if he could, a band that would cross the border and put an end to Turkish atrocities.[39] But men and weapons were hard to come by on such short notice.

Small armed bands of Turks, Serbs, Greeks, Albanians, or Bulgarians were traditional in Macedonia. Every summer, for example, Bulgarian professional bandits, *haramii*, crossed into Turkey from Bulgaria for the purpose of thievery, and in some cases also for personal revenge, returning home in the fall with their booty. Over the years these Bulgarian bandits had built a network of contacts in the villages, enabling them to get food and information on local Turkish troop activity; they also had acquired a thorough knowledge of the mountainous regions and were able to elude pursuit. The *haramii* were well-equipped for their work with modern rifles, ammunition, and adequate clothing. Each member owned his own equipment, and a group could be organized at a moment's notice, unlike the members of IMRO who had to be rounded up, trained, armed, and clothed before they were ready to cross the border.[40]

Unfortunately, the *haramii*, with few exceptions, were not eager to cooperate with the Macedonian movement, much less become members. As early as 1895, Boris Sarafov tried to use *haramii* for revolutionary purposes. As part of the incursion into Macedonia organized by the supreme committee in 1895, Sarafov led a group in an attack on Melnik. Only with the greatest effort did he manage to keep them from looting the city and capturing the local Greek bishop. Variations on this story frequently occurred in the next few years as IMRO tried to use the *haramii* to collect money. As Sarafov noted, "most of them thought only of raising a little ruckus, making sure their money belt didn't remain empty, and not losing their lives, but returning to Bulgaria."[41]

Like the *haramii*, IMRO operated illegally in Macedonia and could do so successfully only by adopting the techniques and the networks of the bandits. Thus, IMRO began to organize temporary bands to achieve a specific purpose: shipment of weapons, collection of money, robbery, or punishment. Totally inexperienced in the clandestine arts or in robbery and kidnapping, and constantly pursued by Turkish soldiers, IMRO's bands had very little success.

Gotse Delchev was the first to organize and lead a band into Macedonia with the express purpose of robbing or kidnapping a rich Turk. His experiences demonstrate the weaknesses and difficulties which IMRO faced in its early years. In 1897, Delchev instructed Nikolai Maleshevsky, the Dupnitsa committee chairman, to train fifteen healthy boys and instill in them the spirit of self-sacrifice to obtain weapons for IMRO.[42] With this band, Delchev crossed into Macedonia in the fall of 1897. In its first attempt, the band surrounded the home of a rich Turk in the district of Kochansko, only to discover that no one was home, and the Turk's riches well-hidden. They then investigated the possibility of kidnapping another Turk who was vacationing in a nearby mineral bath. When that proved impossible, Delchev settled on one Nazlim *bey*, the son of a wealthy landowner in Strumitsa. The band hid for two days by the Strumitsa-

Vasilevo road, waiting for their victim. On the afternoon of the second day, they managed to grab him as he passed. Approximately four days later, the father received a note demanding the delivery of 6,000 *lira* ($24,000) and an end of Turkish patrols in the areas in return for his son.

The patrols stopped, and the father sent 1,500 *lira* with his regards and a request that the smaller sum be accepted because the year was bad, and it was difficult to raise more. Delchev returned the money but agreed to negotiate. On the third Sunday after the kidnapping, the two sides agreed on 3,000 *lira*. That same night, Delchev, racked by the stomach pains which plagued him throughout his life, lay oblivious in one corner of the band's hut, while the rest of the group, except for the guard and the boy, slept. Nazlim *bey* was so loosely bound that he managed to untie himself and seize Delchev's revolver. He asked the guard to take him outside for a minute, and as they left the hut he shot the guard and disappeared into the woods. Nazlim *bey* met the people bringing the ransom to the band, and he returned home with it.[43] Delchev returned to Bulgaria, discouraged and empty-handed. Occupied with organizational work, he did not try again for two years.

In July, 1899 Delchev and another group of young men crossed the border with two other bands that had agreed to help him. One, led by Anton Bozukov, consisted of former non-commissioned officers in the Bulgarian army; the other, led by Kosto Mustruka, were *haramii* whom Delchev was trying to win over to IMRO. Also accompanying him were three members of a young anarchists' society, called the Geneva Group, who agreed to travel with Delchev in return for part of the spoils and a chance to learn something of the political situation in Macedonia.[44]

Mustruka and his band quit Delchev shortly after crossing the border because Delchev insisted that all the money acquired through their combined efforts go to IMRO. Bozukov and his men left a few days later after a political disagreement. Two of the three anarchists deserted shortly afterwards for philosophical reasons. Left with only twelve men, Delchev tried a number of different schemes to raise money. Delchev focussed first on Iliaz *bey*, one of the richest men in the Serres district. Dressed in rags, the unarmed *bey* travelled extensively by himself, but so circuitously that he had never been caught by the many bands who hunted him. Delchev and his band followed the *bey* for over a month but had no more luck in pinning him down than had the professional bandits.

Their next attempt was against a Greek moneylender, Dimitrakis. In a daylight attack on September 8, 1899, they carried Dimitrakis off and hid him from Turkish patrols in the mountains. The band demanded 2.000 *lira* ($8,000) from his brother but received only 180 *lira* with a note saying, "I don't have and can't get more." While negotiations were going on, Delchev left Dimitrakis with part of the band and went off with five men to intercept a large shipment of government money from Nevrokop to Serres. The money, however, was guarded by about sixty-five soldiers, and Delchev could make no attempt to steal it. In the meantime, the rest of the band had forced Dimitrakis to write his brother for more money. While Delchev and the band waited for the additional money to arrive, they arranged local IMRO affairs at a series of meetings. During these meetings, Dimitrakis was always kept apart from the groups so he would not learn of IMRO movements in the area. One night his guard fell asleep, and he escaped to Melnik where he wired his brother to halt payment of the ransom.[45]

It seems reasonably clear that Delchev's failure in these attempts to raise large sums of money quickly was due to three key weaknesses in IMRO at that time: poor organization and discipline; insecure roots in the villages; and unreliable information and supply network. To be effective politically and financially, IMRO not only had to consolidate and organize its present membership, but also had to promote more interest and involvement among the peasantry. To this end, IMRO created as part of each regional committee armed bands which explained and disseminated IMRO's ideas, aims, and orders; prepared IMRO members for a national struggle; organized IMRO committees where none existed; and promoted the idea of "arm yourself."[46] Although not specifically stated, the bands were also expected to do their best to weaken moral and material dependence of the peasantry on Turkish authorities.[47] Through such propaganda activities and through punitive actions against anyone who plagued the Bulgarian population in Macedonia, the bands raised the authority and reputation of IMRO and gave greater concreteness to the revolutionary movement.

IMRO's ability to staff, train, and equip these bands resulted directly from tremendous financial and material help it received from the revived supreme committee in Sofia. In the past, IMRO had refused such help, to preserve its freedom of action. But the May 1899 election of Boris Sarafov as chairman brought significant change to the supreme committee. Under Sarafov's direction, the committee accepted the leading role of IMRO in the revolutionary struggle in Macedonia, and on this basis, IMRO accepted the committee's assistance. From 1899 to 1901, the supreme committee provided subsidies to IMRO's central committee, allowances for Delchev and Petrov in Sofia, and weapons for bands sent to the interior.

Delchev and Petrov were elected full members of the supreme committee. In return, the committee maintained direct communications with IMRO's central committee in Salonika. They cooperated in many ways: in mutual efforts to revive Macedonian friendship societies and clubs throughout Bulgaria and to increase collection of money and weapons from these groups for the interior; through joint workshops producing knapsacks, cartridge belts and other accessories for armed bands; and by the creation of a boarding school in Sofia to train young men, sent by IMRO from Macedonia or recruited in Sofia, in military arts. The supreme committee financed Delchev's foray into Macedonia in 1899; it created and sent bands into Macedonia, which, once across the border, came under IMRO's control.

Sarafov, in his memoirs, claims that by various means, some legal, the supreme committee raised 560,000 leva during his two-year chairmanship.[48] Of that sum, IMRO received 32,927 gold and silver leva in 1899, 77,735 in 1900, and 26,347 between March 25 and April 9, 1901.[49] Petrov admits that without the help of the supreme committee, IMRO would have developed very slowly. In fact, Petrov says, the committee in Sofia was so essential to the growth of IMRO that if it had not existed, "we would have been forced to invent one ourselves." There is no doubt that the financial and material help of the supreme committee enabled IMRO to consolidate and strengthen itself sufficiently to move from agitational work to actual revolutionary activity.

In spite of the close cooperation between the two committees, significant disagreements arose. Spurred by Petrov's and Delchev's suspicions of the sincerity and intentions of the supreme committee's officers, including Sarafov, relations between the two committees seriously deteriorated late in 1900. They held different views of the proper timing and character of the future uprising, when it should be proclaimed, and what role the local population should play. The officers of the supreme committee and their comrades in the Bulgarian army believed that preparations for the uprising were sufficient, with the only obstacle the continual unfitness of IMRO's leaders in the interior, who were mainly schoolteachers, to lead an essentially military operation. To correct that weakness, the supreme committee proposed to send its officers into Macedonia to replace the current leaders. After much debate, the two committees signed a protocol on May 1, 1900, outlining the procedure for assigning officers to IMRO's central committee and to its regional committees.[50] But relations worsened and the protocol was never put into effect.

The supreme committee tried in other ways to absorb IMRO and to gain the leadership of the Macedonian struggle. The decisive rupture between IMRO's representatives in Sofia, Delchev and Petrov on one hand, and the leaders of the supreme committee on the other hand, occurred over the question of correspondence with the central committee in Salonika. The officers assumed that with the inclusion of IMRO's representatives on the staff of the supreme committee, these representatives had neither the need nor the right to maintain a separate channel of communication with the central committee; rather, they should communicate only through the secretary of the supreme committee.[51] Delchev and Petrov, however, feared this would compromise their ability to act as independent agents and would leave IMRO without a spokesman in Bulgaria. All the leading members of IMRO supported the stand of Delchev and Petrov. Petrov continued to write secretly to the central committee. He advised them which supreme committee decisions to heed and which to ignore. When the supreme committee discovered Petrov's activities, they summarily excluded him. Delchev, meanwhile, had already ceased attending committee meetings. In retaliation, the supreme committee cut off all aid to IMRO in January, 1901, and began sending its own bands in Macedonia to agitate against IMRO.

Shortly after breaking with the supreme committee, IMRO suffered an even more devastating blow. In January, 1901, the Ottoman government arrested the entire central committee and exiled them to Asia Minor. When word of their arrest reached the supreme committee, its officers insisted on immediately entering Macedonia and proclaiming the uprising before IMRO's past groundwork could be destroyed by the fierce Turkish repressions which followed the arrests. The determined opposition of Delchev and Petrov, who were now IMRO's de facto leaders, frustrated this plan. Even so, the supreme committee continued to press for an immediate uprising in Macedonia and the two organizations declared open war for control of the Macedonian liberation movement.

IMRO expended enormous amounts of energy and money to maintain its influence against its rival. Especially in the border regions where the supreme committee promised weapons and financial support to those who would join it, the rivalry "wore out people and money in recovering lost territory and holding villages."[52] Increasing defections to the supreme committee of long-standing IMRO members severely strained IMRO's effectiveness and morale. Sir Arthur Biliotti, the British consul in Salonika, described with only slight exaggeration the dilemma facing IMRO, noting "the feeling among the Bulgarian population in Macedonia that while given promises of emancipation, all they had hitherto obtained is imprisonment, bastonade, exile, etc., and that they have nothing substantial to expect from the action of the committee." He went on to say that the leaders would have to prove that "energetic steps" were being taken in order to maintain their adherents in the countryside.[53]

Delchev and Petrov took such steps in March, 1901. In a circular letter sent to all local committees, they announced that the "struggle was entering into a new phase because of two blows which have struck the Internal Organization"—the arrests of the central committee and the decisions and actions of the supreme committee to take over IMRO and begin an armed uprising. The letter warned local committees that while authority was temporarily decentralized, each committee would be held responsible for the outcome of all its actions, and they should avoid any activities that would attract the attention and revenge of Turkish authorities. Finally, the letter commanded committees to tighten discipline and carefully watch the activities of their bands to prevent a premature uprising which would be suicidal for the cause.[54]

At the same time, Delchev and Petrov held a series of meetings with committee chairmen and band leaders, at which they tried to find solutions to IMRO's financial difficulties. At one meeting, Delchev unequivocally refused monetary or material help from the Bulgarian government. He said: "If once you take money from the government under current political conditions, that implies engagements and ties . . . . The Bulgarian government harbors the desire to rule Macedonia. As soon as it begins to provide money, it will know how to use the situation which its help will create and will not be content with a platonic relationship, only with tangible benefits. Moreover, other Balkan and European countries already maintain that the Organization is inspired by Sofia ruling circles . . . . All these considerations force us to look for other means, other sources, always independent of Bulgaria."[55]

At a second meeting in Kiustendil in the summer of 1901, called to discuss "other means," Delchev, Yane Sandansky, and Khristo Chernopeev (the latter two the kidnappers of Ellen Stone), and others agreed that the system of small robberies practised in Samokov, Kiustendil, and Dupnitsa had hurt IMRO's prestige and, in any case, could not keep it financially afloat. Sandansky suggested kidnapping King Ferdinand on one of his many trips to Rila Monastery.[56] Delchev vetoed that suggestion and ordered each band leader to suggest ways to supply money, with the condition that it come from outside Bulgaria. But here they were faced with an unresolvable contradiction. They would not accept aid from Bulgaria, and small-scale projects were unrewarding; yet the circular letter warned that in this delicate period, "large-scale undertakings" or other activities which would "create a lot of noise and provoke persecution by the authorities" must be avoided for the time being. How, then, could IMRO obtain the funds vital for its continued existence?

Of necessity, most members had to ignore the warning, hoping instead that tighter discipline in the bands and the better organization achieved in the countryside would prevent failures of the kind experienced before and, at the same time, lessen the possibility of Turkish revenge. Yane Sandansky and Khristo Chernopeev, so badly equipped that they had to run even from the bands the supreme committee was now sending into the area, determined to kidnap a wealthy Turk in order to ease their desperate financial straits. After careful research, they selected as their victim Suleiman *bey*, the son of the Pasha of Gorna Dzhumaia (present-day Blagoevgrad). They enlisted the help of Sava Mikhailov, a good friend of the *bey* and the Gorna Dzhumaia district chairman, as well as a local schoolteacher, Krüstio Asenov, nephew of the famous liberation fighter, Xadji Dimitür. But before the kidnapping could take place, Suleiman *bey* suffered an incapacitating stroke. Sandansky and Chernopeev had to look elsewhere. After spending a few days arranging IMRO affairs in Gorna Dzhumaia, they left for Bansko to consult with Dimitür Lazarov, the district chairman. There they constructed a plan which would supply IMRO with a tremendous sum of money and popularize the Macedonian movement throughout Europe and the United States.

Chapter II
Planning and Execution of the Kidnapping

Bansko had both a thriving Protestant church and an active IMRO chapter; Dimitür Lazarov, chairman of the local IMRO committee, was also a Protestant. He was one of a number of Protestant members of IMRO, all of whom were well-regarded and highly trusted. P. K. Yavorov noted that as members of IMRO, Protestants were more zealous and capable than their Orthodox counterparts.[1] Exactly who suggested to Sandansky and Chernopeev that they kidnap a missionary instead of a Turk is not clear, since several people claim that honor.[2] The target initially selected was Dr. John House, who was to be invited to Bansko by one of the local Protestants and seized there. Sandansky and Chernopeev learned that House refused to travel in the area because it was too dangerous, but an American woman missionary, Ellen Stone, was in Bansko at that very time.

Ellen Stone was in Bansko to conduct a two-week training and refresher course for local teachers in the Protestant primary schools and for "Bible women" who worked under the auspices of the mission station at Salonika. Born of religious parents, in Roxbury, Massachusetts, in 1846, Stone taught school for two years in Chelsea, Massachusetts, before joining the editorial staff of the *Boston Congregationalist*. As her religious convictions deepened, she offered her services to the American Board of Commissioners for Foreign Missions, which assigned her to the Girls' School in Samokov, Bulgaria, in 1878. Because of disagreements with the director of the school, Stone was transferred in 1883 to Plovdiv. She spent much of the next ten years visiting women in their homes, teaching reading and rudimentary hygienics, and propagandizing Protestant Christianity. At the same time she began to train a corps of native "Bible women" to perform similar work. She took charge of the Plovdiv Girls' School for a time and also travelled to Sofia during 1885 to minister to the casualties of the Serbian-Bulgarian War. In 1898, after a brief trip to the United States, she was assigned to the Salonika Mission Station and placed in charge of evangelical work for women in that area. Her new job required much touring throughout Protestant communities in Macedonia, most of them in isolated, rural mountainous areas.

Stone had, according to her memoirs, a few trifling brushes with the bandits infesting Macedonia: once she spent the night in the common room of an inn with a brigand sleeping on the side of the fire; another time, bandits stole two horses from the party with which she was travelling; and once two bandits stopped her on the road but allowed her to pass unmolested.[3] These encounters made her conscious of the dangers of touring, but, as she had travelled the road from Bansko to Gorna Dzhumaia many times, she did not fear the trip. In fact, familiarity with the people of the area and their ways gave her a distinct feeling of security. On this latest trip to Bansko, Stone travelled to a number of villages in the Razlog district accompanied by a class of eight women, to familiarize them with Protestant activities in the field and to inspire confidence in the local Protestants.

The decision to seize Miss Stone was not an easy one for Sandansky and Chernopeev. She was, after all, a woman in her fifties who might not survive the hazardous flight through the mountains. Besides, the morality of the times forced the band to capture a female companion for Stone in order to preserve her reputation. But Sandansky and Chernopeev in desperation convinced themselves that Stone deserved to be kidnapped because she "preached against the *cheta* [armed bands], saying God would right the trouble of the poor peasants, not the *chetas*." Thus, with some reluctance, they proceeded, believing that the Turkish government would be forced to pay a ransom quickly in order to avoid international complications.[4]

Sandansky and Chernopeev set about getting official permission from local and central committees for their plan.[5] Sava Mikhailov went to Sofia to ask Delchev and Petrov, while Sandansky and Chernopeev travelled from Bansko to Razlog and back again seeking authorization from the local regional committee. It was not easy to get the unanimous approval of the plan that Lazarov insisted they obtain. The five local committee members, two of whom were Protestants, feared not only for the safety of Miss Stone, but also for the safety of their families and property, which would be endangered by Turkish reprisals. Only with great reluctance did they accept the kidnapping plan, convinced by Lazarov of IMRO's desperate financial straits.[6]

By the time Sandansky and Chernopeev got the necessary unanimous consent, they faced a revolt among the members of their band who, since the unsuccessful attempt on Suleiman *bey*, had been hiding from Turkish patrols in the Pirin mountains, without any communication from Sandansky or Chernopeev. Sandansky got a letter from the temporary leader, Nikolai Dechev, saying the band would return to Bulgaria unless Sandansky and Chernopeev appeared before the band immediately. Whatever caused the unrest—hunger, cold, fear of Turkish patrols, or Dechev's distrust of Sandansky and Chernopeev and desire to lead a band himself—the letter was an ultimatum to which Sandansky and Chernopeev responded at once. Collecting seven armed men from Bansko, they travelled all day before they found the band. Sandansky and Chernopeev were willing to free from their obligations those malcontents who wanted to return to Bulgaria, but they insisted that those returning leave their weapons behind. During the ensuing quarrel, eleven of the fourteen band members were disarmed and escorted back to Bulgaria by a special courier. Sandansky and Chernopeev retained only three men in their band just a week before Ellen Stone was to leave Bansko.

The small band headed for Vlakhi (Sandansky's birthplace) to rest and recruit new members. On route, they were summoned urgently to Bansko by a messenger sent by a member of the regional committee. Two committee members had changed their minds and refused to support the kidnapping. Sandansky and Chernopeev rushed back to Bansko, where the two dissenters pleaded with them to drop the plan, because "we will burn; it will arouse affairs unseen until now in our villages and throughout Razlog and Dospat."[7]

Chernopeev responded that sacrifices are a necessary and inevitable result of the struggle for the liberation of Macedonia; unless the dissenters were each willing to give IMRO 500 *lira*, the kidnapping would take place because the cause required money. Sandansky reassured the committee that the kidnapping would take place as far outside Bansko as possible to save the town from Turkish revenge. Thus appeased, the committee once again gave its approval on the condition that the kidnapping take place on the road from Razlog to Gorna Dzhumaia (about 15 kilometers from Bansko), and that the kidnappers wear Turkish disguises and speak only Turkish to fool the authorities.

In the few days remaining before Stone was to leave Bansko, the band recruited additional members and planned the capture. Dimitür Lazarov secured an introduction to Stone through the priest of the Bansko evangelical church and learned the date and approximate time of her departure. The band resolved to lie in ambush at a place called "Leaning Cliff," where they would be warned of Stone's approach by a man wearing a white handkerchief on his head. They asked a local Protestant to join the band temporarily in order to identify Stone and assigned three trustworthy IMRO members as drivers for the Stone party.

As the day of Stone's departure neared, Mikhailov returned from Bulgaria with Krŭstio Asenov and additional band members, but without the essential approval of Delchev and Petrov. They refused to believe that a large ransom could be obtained for Stone, and they felt her kidnapping would evoke severe Turkish reprisals. While Delchev hesitated, Petrov vetoed the plan as too dangerous; nevertheless, Sandansky and Chernopeev determined to carry on, assuming personal responsibility for the outcome.[8]

September 3, 1901, according to Stone, was clear, warm and bright—a "perfect September day."[9] Stone, Katerina Usheva and her son Peter, Katerina Tsilka and her husband Grigor, three young female teachers, and two classmates of Peter Usheva at the Protestant school planned to travel together to Gorna Dzhumaia, where the party would split up: Stone would go to Salonika, the Tsilkas to Kortcha in Albania, the others to Samokov, Sofia, Bitola, and elsewhere. Farewells took a little longer than usual because none of the members of the caravan planned to return to Bansko for a number of months, but finally, covered with flowers bestowed by well-wishers, they rode out of Bansko. Accompanied by three drivers, they stopped to picnic and enjoy the coolness of the forest; therefore it was after 5:00 P.M. when they reached the "Leaning Cliff." Stone recalled the place as an admirable spot for an ambush: "A bald crag of the mountain which juts out into the valley, turning the stream to one side. At this point the pathway leads down into the water, so that travelers must ride into the swift current, pass around the rock, and strike the trail again on the farther side."

Sandansky, Chernopeev, and their band of twenty men had waited anxiously all day. They had disguised themselves carefully: five were dressed in Turkish military uniforms, and the others in ragged, nondescript garments. With blackened faces and heads covered with rags, they were almost unrecognizable. At last they spotted a man with a white handkerchief on his head. Shortly thereafter the first member of the caravan rounded the jutting rock; the band scrambled out of hiding, screaming in Turkish. The startled caravan was surrounded by armed men who "seemed to have sprung from the hillside"; men who frantically demanded that the caravaners dismount and surrender. The captured party, pushed and pulled by the band, stumbled through the stream and crawled up the steep cliff opposite the road. Shouts of "Hurry!" and waving of guns urged them on, for Sandansky and Chernopeev were extremely afraid of being seen by a passing traveller or of being heard by Turkish guards posted a few kilometers back on the road to Razlog.

"Driven like cattle" during a two-hour climb, the exhausted travellers were finally allowed to collapse in a small clearing near the peak, Popova Glava. There they were ordered to wait while Sandansky killed an unfortunate Turk who, passing the "Leaning Cliff" minutes before the caravan, had been seized.[10] Then Sandansky motioned for Stone to step forward; with "indescribable horror" she obeyed and, much to her surprise, was commanded to wait up the slope away from her companions.

The travellers, expecting to be robbed, had carefully hidden their money and other valuables. Grigor Tsilka gave his wife his pocket watch and money; she put the money in her mouth and hid the watch carefully under her belt. But the watch chain showed out and, to her amazement, a member of the band warned her that it was showing and advised her to conceal it better. The band disregarded all valuables as they searched the luggage and took every scrap of food they could find, plus a Bible from one of the young teachers. Their actions mystified the travellers; if the bandits did not want money, what did they want? And if they were Turks as they appeared to be, why did they kill a Turk, and why did they ravenously consume the pork products along with other food?[11] An answer to the first question was not long in coming. In a hurried conference, Sandansky and Chernopeev decided that Mrs. Ushev was too old and frail to be taken as Stone's companion, as they had originally planned. Besides, at that point, she was suffering from terrible stomach cramps brought on by eating too much honey at lunch. The only other married woman was Katerina Tsilka; she was sent up the slope to join Stone.

Tsilka was five months pregnant. She had been in Bansko visiting her parents whom she had not seen in nine years, and there she had buried her only child, a son who died suddenly. Mr. and Mrs. Tsilka were graduates of American Protestant schools—hers in Samokov, his in Monastir. They had met and married in New York, where she had studied first at Northfield Academy and then at the Training School of Nurses of New York Presbyterian Hospital, and he had attended

Union Theological Seminary. On their return from the United States, Grigor Tsilka had established a parish in Kortcha, Albania.

The travellers wailed and sobbed as Sandansky, Chernopeev, and five of the band motioned Tsilka and Stone to follow them. The other travellers, surrounded by guards, watched helplessly as the two were led quickly up and over a sharp rise to the south. The women, armed only with a Bible and an umbrella, and dressed in light summer clothing, were wholly unprepared for the odyssey they now embarked on, and they were deeply puzzled about its purposes.

The band released the other travellers next morning and instructed them to tell the authorities that Turkish-speaking bandits had captured Stone and Tsilka. In one last effort to reinforce the impression that Turks had been responsible for the deed, the part of the band left behind dressed two of its members as women. Heading north, they travelled through a number of Muslim villages around Babek, towing the "two women" along.

* * * * *

Stone and Tsilka climbed a steep incline south of where their travelling companions remained. Stumbling and panting, they reached the top of Popova Glava, where two sturdy horses awaited them. Puzzled as to why the "brigands" had carried them away, the two women questioned their captors, whose only response, a far from reassuring one, was: "Do not be afraid, we won't do anything." As if to convince the ladies of their sincerity, members of the band gave them a shawl and a heavy cloak as protection from the mountain's cool night.

It was a strange procession through the mountains. A middle-aged American woman and a young Bulgarian woman, swaying on their horses; ten or so "brigands," rifles slung over their backs, goat-hair capes dragging on the ground, marching in utter silence in front and back of the women. One of the band, Krüstio Asenov, better known as "the bear" because of his tremendous size, walked ahead cutting branches and uprooting young trees to clear a path through the thickly wooded forest. The group wove in and out of the forest, changing directions often to confuse any trackers. Sometimes they heard dogs barking, sometimes sheep baaing; sometimes they caught a glimpse of a shepherd's hut.

Exhausted by the day's events, Stone fell off her horse at one point and felt content just to lie on the cold ground and rest; but, denied that pleasure, she was immediately lifted back on her horse.

Later, after much pleading, the band allowed the women to stop for a rest. They spread capes on the ground for the women, who fell sound asleep before they had a chance to cover themselves. Soon they were lifted back into their saddles. Shortly before dawn they arrived at a very steep cliff which they had to descend by goat paths. Unable to descend on the horses and too tired to walk themselves, the women were carried down in turn on the back of Asenov. By dawn, they arrrived in a desolate, heavily vegetated ravine surrounded by jagged peaks, near the village of Dolna Sushitsa. The band, satisfied that no one could see or hear them, spread a wool blanket for the women and announced that the group would spend the day there and travel again at night.

The band did its best to make Stone and Tsilka comfortable. They cut branches to make the women a shelter and brought them more food than they could possibly eat; fresh milk, remains of the food that the caravan had been carrying, including pastry baked by Tsilka's mother, a special type of dried pork, pears, tart berries, and clear spring water. The women were particularly touched by a bouquet of wild cyclamen, which one of the band gathered because he saw that the flowers from the previous day's farewells had faded. The women were doubly reassured of the good intentions of their captors when one of them produced the schoolteacher's Bible. The behavior of their captors convinced Stone and Tsilka that they had not been brought to this lonely spot to be killed. How could someone bring you flowers and then dispatch you with his knife? They still expected to be robbed, however, and carefully hid their valuables while no one was looking. A chance remark during the previous night's journey led them to suspect that they had been seized for reasons more important than the contents of their pockets. During an especially difficult stretch of the journey, when the women had to be helped to stay on their horses by members of the band, they heard some band members complain about the dangers of Turkish troops and the difficulty of travelling fast with two women along; these men had been reassured by others that the *lira* received would make it worth the trouble.

The women spent the rest of the first day mending torn garments with a huge needle and coarse thread supplied by one of the band— Stone even resewed the decorative braid which had come off her skirt during her crawl up the mountain; they washed themselves and slept. The band generally refused to converse with the women, but what little conversation did pass was in Bulgarian. Stone spoke about her ninety-year-old mother and four brothers who would be heart-broken if anything happened to her, and about God who would "love and care for all his children." Most of her speech went unnoticed, although Sandansky did agree that "we are all God's children," convincing Stone that at least there was one Christian among her captors.

Late in the afternoon, a band member brought the women a half-boiled chicken. He apologized profusely for the haphazard cooking and for his lateness in arriving, but explained that the peasant who had been asked to prepare a chicken had boiled it with ten hot peppers and two and a half pounds of flour. Cooked this way the chicken was inedible even for the members of the band, and the peasant had to cook another one. The women gratefully wrapped the chicken and the leftover scraps of food in a white cloth and packed it together with their Bible and shawl in goat-hair bags the band had given them.

By dusk the group left the ravine and headed up to the peaks towering above them. They went on foot because the goat and sheep paths were too narrow and steep for the horses, and soon the exhausted women had to be half-dragged, half-carried to the top, where they were allowed to remount. The journey was long and difficult, as the band was intent on getting as far away as possible from the scene of the kidnapping. Heading east, they scrambled up sharp inclines and descended through the underbrush. Although they crossed a few roads, there was no possibility of travelling on them. The women had only one or two pauses for rest and a few sips of buttermilk, which magically appeared out of an earthen jar, before they were commanded to dismount and wait for a few minutes. Part of the band disappeared, to return with two heavy goat-hair hooded cloaks which they draped over the women so they could see nothing but the ground at their feet. They were led through a long, narrow door into a dark, damp, one-room hut with a small, barred window, and they were told they could rest here during the day before travelling again at night.

In this hovel, near the village of Padezh, Stone and Tsilka passed a wretched day, exhausted but unable to sleep. They returned the half-boiled chicken to be cooked and contented themselves with a little bread and cheese. Certain that they would be killed in this place, the women complained and cried, and demanded to know who their kidnappers were. The answer, "Among us are Turks and others," did not satisfy them.

Shortly before the band left for its third night of travel, Sandansky, Chernopeev, and Asenov filed into the hovel, armed from head to toe, with cartridges around their chest and waist, daggers and revolvers on their hips. The three had left their rifles outside, but Asenov soon brought them in and stacked them in a corner. Stone and Tsilka saw the rifles as further evidence of their helplessness, although Sandansky, Chernopeev, and Asenov probably meant only to ensure that the rifles were not damaged by the weather. Stone and Tsilka forgot the stale air and the terrible smell of long-unwashed clothing when Chernopeev began to speak. He was convinced that the women would cooperate better if they were terrified and tried to frighten them as much as possible. Chernopeev was dirty, ragged, and ill-mannered, appearing capable of carrying out any threat. In a harsh voice he declared, we are bandits and have captured you for ransom. If we do not receive the money quickly we will kill you without mercy. If you try to escape you will be shot immediately. Stone, contemptuous of these three ill-smelling men who "were at no pains to remove their fezes from their heads," haughtily informed them that neither she nor Tsilka would make it easier for the band by escaping, and if anything happened to either one of the women, the brigands would answer to God.

The band ignored Stone's remarks, and she forgot her disdain when she heard the amount of ransom money the band was asking: 25.000 *lira*—$100,000! Neither Stone nor Tsilka could conceive of so much money, much less imagine where it could be obtained. As Sandansky, Chernopeev, and Asenov left the room, the two women realized the danger of their position and were convinced that their captors might just as well kill them now because the ransom could never be paid. Death now would certainly be better than riding the horses on another trek through the wild mountains.

According to Chernopeev, the band had decided to hold the women for a month in the belief that the ransom would arrive from Constantinople within a week of its publication. They, of course, never intended to kill the women, but the women did not realize their threats were empty bluffs and prayed continually for God's help. Stone also tried a more practical tactic of convincing Chernopeev and Sandansky that neither she nor Tsilka had money. Both were from poor families and as "humble Christian workers and daughters of the people" had no way of raising $100,000, or anything approaching it. She informed them that the American Board for which she worked had declared a few years before that it would not ransom any of its members if they fell into the hands of bandits. Rational arguments gave way to wailing and pleading, with as little effect. Sandansky and Chernopeev were not going to give up.

The third night the band crossed the border into Bulgaria, passing east of Gorna Dzhumaia, near Frolop. Chernopeev and Asenov had arranged the crossing the day before from Padezh. The band planned to stay in Bulgaria only until the furor died down and then return to the Gorna Dzhumaia area. As they ascended a steep hill by the border, the saddle-girth on Tsilka's horse broke, and she tumbled off with a scream, the saddle landing on top of her. Stone jumped down to help her, while the band stood motionless, petrified that one of the Turkish border guards had heard her cry. The panic-stricken Tsilka could do no more than sob quietly and refuse to stand up. Members of the band gently picked up Tsilka, brushed her off, and reseated her on her horse.

Dawn brought them to a heavy forest, where they dismounted and spent the day near the house of an IMRO member. Asenov and Chernopeev were dispatched to Tservishte to find safe accommodations. The next day Sandansky and the others smuggled the women into the house Asenov and Chernopeev had picked out. Sandansky then left for Dupnitsa to see a doctor because he had dislocated a bone in his foot during the strenuous climbs of the past few days.

The band considered themselves safe in Tservishte because the authorities, both Bulgarian and Turkish, fooled by the decoy band travelling to Batak, were searching for them elsewhere. But Sandansky learned in Dupnitsa that Bulgarian patrols were beginning active searches of all border villages, not just those further east. Cutting short his stay in Dupnitsa, even though his foot was not yet healed, Sandansky rushed back to Tservishte. The band decided to retreat to to the mountainous Gorna Dzhumaia area, where they could hide more easily from patrols. They crossed back into Turkey by the same route as they had come with the help of the villagers of Frolop in Bulgaria and Drianovo in Turkey. Without stopping, the band passed through Leshko and finally arrived in Selishte. It was there on September 9, six days after the kidnapping, that Asenov, Chernopeev, and Sandansky advised Stone the time had come for her to write her letter to the outside world. They handed her paper, pen, and ink and dictated what she was to write. They let her choose any person to write to who lived in Bansko. She chose Konstantin Petkanchin, a member of the Protestant church and an old friend. The letter (which is not preserved) informed him that she and Tsilka had been captured by highwaymen who were demanding 25,000 *lira* and were prepared to kill the women if they did not get the money within twenty days. She entrusted Petkanchin with conducting necessary negotiations and with personally notifying William Peet, the treasurer of the American Board in Constantinople, of their situation. The three leaders carefully checked the letter, written in Bulgarian; they collected the leftover paper, ink, and the pen and left the hut.

For eleven days the band and their captives waited in that area for a response, moving once to Pokrovnik and then back to Selishte. Although Stone and Tsilka were never told, it seems the courier had not been able to deliver Stone's letter to Petkanchin in person, but had left it lying on his doorstep. Petkanchin was so terrified of being identified with a revolutionary group and thus incurring the wrath of the Turkish authorities that he ignored the letter.

The band blamed the women for the failure to open negotiations. Asenov, Chernopeev, and Sandansky, looking especially sinister and violent, crowded into the storage room where the women were hidden to demand that Stone write a second letter. The three decided that a quicker response would be gained from a fellow American missionary and that direct delivery of a letter could be more easily accomplished in Bulgaria. They ordered Stone to pick a Protestant missionary in Samokov and instruct him to go personally to Constantinople to give Peet a letter demanding the ransom. Peet, in turn, was instructed to request through the American minister in Constantinople a cessation of Turkish troop movements, on the grounds that any encounter with the Turks would almost certainly cause the deaths of Stone and Tsilka.

With the three men standing over her, Stone wrote to the Reverend H. C. Haskell that she and Tsilka were suffering terrible deprivations, and that Tsilka was pregnant and could not stand more travel. She begged him to do all in his power to convince Peet and other members of the American Board that the bandits were prepared to kill them if they did not receive 25,000 *lira*, the money to be brought to Bansko where the band would arrange to pick it up. The three men allowed her to add eighteen days to the time limit, but refused to let her add a message of her own. They also rejected Stone's plea that an initial payment of "earnest money" be allowed. Resignedly, Stone did what they commanded, writing in addition an authorization which Tsilka countersigned, authorizing the bearer of the note to collect the full sum requested for their ransom.

Although Stone's letter described their captors as merciless and their situation as desperate, in reality she and Tsilka received very good treatment, as good as could be expected from a group of men constantly one step ahead of Turkish patrols. Sava Mihkailov stated in his memoirs that IMRO had collected a good deal of money in the interior, which they were going to use to buy weapons for their supporters. Instead, they spent all the money supporting Stone and Tsilka, and the promised weapons never got delivered.[13] The women never lacked food. In fact, Stone bemoaned the fact that while she and Tsilka longed for freedom, all they got was a polite, "What would you like for dinner or supper?" From a list that Stone and Tsilka drew up, the band supplied them with underwear and men's socks, material for handkerchiefs and two blouses, needles, thimbles, and thread. The band took special care of Tsilka after Stone informed them she was pregnant. There was always somebody ready to help her mount and dismount, to offer an arm on steep slopes, or even to carry her when the trail got rough. The brigands prepared a bed for the women every night and sometimes even tucked them in.

Stone's second letter had been entrusted to a second carrier. Some say Asenov personally delivered it, although no one is sure. One of the missionaries spotted a stranger near the American School in Samokov asking for one of the students who had travelled with a band previously, but the stranger disappeared before the missionary could ask his name or business.[14] All that is certain is that around 11 P.M. on September 24, 1901, a tall, well-dressed stranger knocked on Haskell's daughter's bedroom window, shoved the letter through the window when she opened it, and disappeared. Haskell left immediately for Constantinople, arriving on September 28 for meetings with Peet and the American chargé d'affaires, Eddy.

Chapter III
First Diplomatic Efforts to Release Stone

Dr. John House, the senior missionary in Macedonia, was the first foreigner to learn of the kidnapping in a telegram from the local Protestant pastor in Razlog, Sedloeff. At dawn on September 4, 1901, after the band guarding Stone and Tsilka's travelling companions departed, the travellers carefully picked their way back on the road, collecting clothes, books, and blankets which had fallen off or been discarded during the mad scramble up the mountain. The three boys headed for Samokov, while Grigor Tsilka and the four ladies returned to Bansko to notify the authorities. Passing through Razlog, they asked Sedloeff to telegraph House in Salonika. House received the wire about 1:00 A.M. on September 5 and went immediately to the American consul, P. H. Lazzaro, who dispatched a message to Charles Dickinson, the American consul general in Constantinople.

On the same day, Lazzaro also informed the *Vali* (the governor of Salonika Province), who blamed Stone for not taking a guard with her. The points Lazzaro made in his interview with the *Vali*, and later in his first report to Dickinson, were to be repeated over and over by the Americans dealing with the Turks. Lazzaro extracted a promise from the *Vali* that Turkish troops would make no attempt to rescue the women or capture the band by force, as they were inclined to. In earlier kidnappings, such actions always led to the death of the captives. With Lazzaro watching, the *Vali* wired the *Mutessarif* (the county head) of Serres, instructing him to dispatch troops to the area of the kidnapping, but only for the purpose of surveillance. Lazzaro's telegram to Dickinson advised him to inform the Porte directly of the danger of sending troops and noted that it was customary in such cases for the Porte to pay the ransom. However, because of the penurious state of the Porte's treasury, the foreign government involved usually had advanced the ransom money and had been reimbursed later. Lazzaro hoped the American government would understand this process and set aside a certain sum in order to be ready when the ransom demand was published.[1]

Local Turkish authorities reacted swiftly to the kidnapping but had little success in tracing the kidnappers or learning their identity. They interrogated all members of the caravan, particularly Grigor Tsilka whom they suspected of being involved in the kidnapping. At the same time, Turkish police arrested the three muleteers but released them without learning anything. They then focused their attention on the Pomak villages around Batak, arresting and imprisoning a few Bulgarian Muslims, also to no avail. Convinced that the Protestants had worked together with IMRO on the kidnapping, the local authorities in Razlog and Gorna Dzhumaia detained most of the committee members in Bansko—Dimitur Lazarov, Boris and Georgi Todev, Ivan Bitanov—and a number of local Protestants, including Tsilka's father, releasing them only after the English consul general in Salonika, Alfred Biliotti, interceded on their behalf. Thorough house-to-house searches in the Razlog-Bansko area were also carried out, and all the mountain passes near the border were cleared of local inhabitants and manned with soldiers.

The Bulgarian government, without being asked by the Turks or the Americans, quickly set about strengthening border patrols to prevent the band from crossing into Bulgaria. The Bulgarian government had learned of the kidnapping on September 5 in a telegram from the Bulgarian commercial agent in Salonika, Anton Shopov. Shopov briefly summarized the known facts and advised that orders be given to border guards to capture the brigands if they tried to cross the border. The Ministry of Foreign Affairs transmitted Shopov's message on September 6 to the Defense Ministry and the Ministry of Internal Affairs so that the necessary steps could be taken.[2] Patrols were stepped up in the regions of Samokov, Dupnitsa, and Geleo, and agents were dispatched to question the missionaries in Samokov and the three young men who had been travelling with Stone and Tsilka. In addition, woodcutters and shepherds inhabiting the border area were ordered to move further into the interior to prevent them from supporting the band if it succeeded in passing the border.

There was not much anyone could do until a request for ransom was published, and they spent the first few weeks trying to identify the kidnappers. Although the Sofia newspaper, *Vechernia Poshta*, claimed the kidnappers were disbanded or deserted soldiers, the released members of the caravan insisted the kidnappers were Bulgarians, not Turks. In interviews with Turkish authorities and American missionaries, the travellers stressed that the kidnappers spoke poor

Turkish but good Bulgarian, that they eagerly consumed the pork
and ham the party was carrying, and that they cold-bloodedly had
killed a Turk. In addition, the kidnapping took place in an area where
Bulgarians were the predominant population, and Turkish and Albanian bands traditionally did not capture women.[3] It also seemed
reasonably clear that the kidnapping had been planned in advance
and that Stone was the intended target.

Exactly who these Bulgarian kidnappers were was disputed vigorously in the diplomatic corps in Salonika and Constantinople and
among the missionaries. Most of the Bulgarian press supported the
theory that the group was composed of Turkish soldiers, while the
Turkish government and the American minister to Constantinople,
John Leishman, believed they were Bulgarian bandits, organized and
armed in Bulgaria for the purpose of kidnapping Stone and collecting a ransom.[4] The missionaries, most of the diplomats in Salonika,
and James McGregor, the British chargé d'affaires in Sofia, were convinced that the kidnapping had political as well as monetary motive.[5]
According to this third theory, the kidnappers had been aided by the
Macedonian Committee in Sofia (and possibly directed by Boris
Sarafov, the former head of the supreme committee), hoping through
the kidnapping to show that Macedonia was unsafe and Turkish control nonexistent. Moreover, the missionaries believed the kidnapping
was in revenge for their failure to support the Macedonian cause in
the past and was intended to provoke foreign intervention in Macedonian affairs.[6] There was one more theory, more ridiculous than
most, held by some of the Turkish authorities, that Stone and Tsilka
had had a hand in their own kidnapping, either because of their sym-
pathies for the Macedonian revolutionaries or because they expected
to acquire a large part of the ransom for themselves,[7] but this theory
was regarded as so preposterous that it was never transmitted to the
Bulgarian Foreign Ministry or the American State Department.

No one knew where the band was and why the ransom demand
was delayed. Lazzaro, in his first report to Dickinson, expressed the
belief that Tsilka was taken along with Stone to act as a negotiator
and would soon be released, together with the ransom demand.[8]
Leishman reported to the State Department on September 20 and
24 that the delay in releasing Tsilka and starting negotiations was
due to active pursuit of the band by Turkish soldiers (even though
the *Vali* had promised to hold the soldiers back) and the inability of
the band to settle down and negotiate. He added that it was possible
that the three muleteers whom the Turks had arrested had brought a

ransom demand which the "Porte found so outrageous, it was attempting to negotiate without U.S. pressure to give in."[9]

The question of where the band was hiding was bitterly argued. By the time of Leishman's September 24 report, it was broadly assumed, except by the Bulgarians who insisted their border was impenetrable, that the band was in Bulgaria. In the first week or so after the capture, however, a number of locations were mentioned. The Turks, at first agreeing that the band was still in Turkey, at one point even claimed to have them surrounded by 2,000 soldiers in the Pirin mountains near the Bulgarian border. But, they asserted, because the soldiers were prevented from moving overtly against the band by American wishes, the band escaped. The Turks, apparently foiled by the decoy band travelling in Batak, then insisted that the band was headed for Roumelia. Shortly after that, the *Vali* informed Lazzaro that the women were being kept near Melnik, while at the same time, the Ottoman imperial commissioner in Sofia was insisting to the Bulgarian government that they were hiding in Rila Monastery.[10]

On the basis of the imperial commissioner's report, which was supported by American missionaries, Leishman informed the State Department that the band was in Bulgaria.[11] In a number of interviews with Ivan St. Gueshov, the Bulgarian diplomatic agent in Constantinople, Leishman questioned the efficacy of measures taken by the Bulgarian government, but Gueshov repeatedly assured him that the Bulgarians were moving vigorously to prevent the band from crossing the border. Even though the Bulgarian commercial agent, Shopov, had reported the belief of some Bulgarians living in Razlog that the band was hiding in some village on the Bulgarian side of the border, the Bulgarian government maintained publicly that the band was in Turkey.[12] In retrospect, it seems clear that the Bulgarian government was usually correct in its view that the band was in Turkey, but, at the time, no one believed it.

*   *   *   *   *

Ellen Stone was the first American kidnapped outside the continental United States. Moreover, she was a woman and part of the powerful religious sector of the American population. It was only natural that her cause was championed by the American public and, as a result, by the American government. The State Department took an immediate interest in the kidnapping; it released the news to the American Board in Boston and to the press, and wired Leishman in

Constantinople to do everything possible for Stone. In subsequent reports to the department, Leishman and Dickinson relayed various rumors on the identity of the kidnappers, their whereabouts, and Bulgarian and Turkish government activities. Leishman asked and received permission to urge the Porte to restrain its troops in order to protect Stone. The State Department chose not to deal with the ransom question but instead instructed Leishman to represent to the Porte the American government's deep concern for Stone's welfare and its view of consequences which would follow her death. Such representations were meant to remind the Porte of its responsibility for the affair and keep it from rash actions which could jeopardize Stone's life.

At the time of the kidnapping, American interests in Bulgaria were represented by the English Legation in Sofia as they had been since Bulgaria's liberation. The United States and Bulgaria had agreed on the establishment of diplomatic relations early in 1901, and Dickinson had been accepted in principle as the American agent in Sofia by the Bulgarian government. Dickinson, already consul general in Constantinople, took the oath of office as diplomatic agent to Sofia on July 3, 1901, and shortly thereafter sent his letter of credence to the Bulgarian Minister of Foreign Affairs, expressing the hope that he would be received officially by Prince Ferdinand.

Dickinson nourished great plans to develop American trade with the principality, for he firmly believed that Bulgarians had tremendous interest in American goods and technology. Even before he received an answer from the Bulgarian Foreign Ministry, he requested permission from the State Department to establish consular agents to promote American business in the major cities of the principality. In fact, Dickinson believed that with "such a strong Bulgarian sentiment in favor of American business, commercial work would overshadow any diplomatic functions and make official recognition [of his and his consular agents' status] by Ferdinand unnecessary."[13]

It took almost two months for the Bulgarians to reply to Dickinson's letter of credence. On August 31 (18 August in the old calendar), Ivan Gueshov, the Bulgarian agent in Constantinople, informed Dickinson in writing that his appointment was agreeable to Prince Ferdinand, on the condition that Dickinson "break off all relations with the consulate general of the United States in Constantinople" and "establish permanent residence in Sofia" because it is "incompatible in principle to have an accumulation on your part" of the two functions."[14]

Although the State Deparment received Gueshov's letter, the conditions it set were not observed: possibly because the department assumed that since the Bulgarian government had agreed to Dickinson's appointment in principle, the matter was not serious; possibly because the Stone affair intervened, and there was not time to obtain agreement for a different diplomatic agent. In any event, at least until the end of the Stone affair, the department considered Dickinson its agent to the Bulgarian government, which, although it never officially accredited Dickinson, treated him as a legitimate representative of the American government in Sofia.[15]

American attention focussed on Turkey during the first few weeks after the kidnapping; hence it was not deemed necessary for Dickinson to go in person to Sofia. Instead, James McGregor, chargé d'affaires of the British Legation in Sofia, was asked to inform the Bulgarian government of American concern and secure Bulgarian cooperation. On September 15, McGregor saw St. Danev, the Minister of Foreign Affairs, to inform him of the kidnapping, relay the view of the United States government that the kidnappers were Bulgarians, and request increased border guards. Danev assured McGregor that measures had already been taken to prevent the band from crossing into Bulgaria. McGregor then voiced his own suspicions that the kidnapping had been the work of a secret committee in Macedonia abetted by Boris Sarafov, and warned Danev not to let Sarafov leave the country as he planned, according to McGregor's information.

After two attempts to see the Minister of Internal Affairs, Mikhail Sarafov (no relation to Boris), McGregor met with the acting secretary general of the Ministry of Foreign Affairs and aide to Prince Ferdinand, Vernazza. Repeating the points made in his conversation with Danev, McGregor, again on his own initiative, added that the United State government would hold the Bulgarian government morally responsible for the disappearance of Boris Sarafov. On September 19, McGregor at last saw Mikhail Sarafov and told him that the band and its captives were in the Rila mountains (information he had received from the imperial Ottoman commissioner in Sofia). Sarafov promised to warn police in that area but he refused to arrest Boris Sarafov or to prevent him from leaving the country in the absence of concrete proof of his involvement in the kidnapping. The minister insisted that Boris Sarafov was discredited with the Macedonian Supreme Committee and could not have been involved. In relaying this information to Leishman in Constantinople, McGregor added his own view that the Bulgarian government was reluctant to take any action and that Boris Sarafov had still many followers in the countryside who could have carried out the kidnapping.[16]

McGregor's readiness to believe the worst of the Bulgarian government and his suspicions of Bulgarian actions were not peculiar to him alone. Bulgaria had had a "poor press" in most of Europe since the Treaty of San Stefano in 1878, and in the Stone affair, most diplomats and others involved tended to demand a level of responsibility and activity from the Bulgarian government which would have been justified only by real evidence of official or semi-official complicity in the kidnapping. There was no such evidence, but McGregor and others took hearsay and rumor as its equivalent and pressed their demands.[17]

The official position of the Bulgarian government never changed, although tendentious press reporting, the diplomatic rumor mill, and foreigners' misunderstanding of the true nature of the Macedonian movement, constantly put it on the defensive. The Foreign Ministry did its best to point out that an alliance-cum-plot between a "secret Macedonian Committee" and Boris Sarafov was completely unlikely, given the animosity between Sarafov and IMRO. The ministry rejected the imputation of blame to the Bulgarian state, pointing out that the crime took place in Turkey and not in Bulgaria.[18] According to a senior member of the government, even if the kidnapping had been planned in Bulgaria (which was not then proved), to say that Bulgaria must therefore bear responsibility would be tantamount to holding the United States responsible for assassinations attempted in Europe by American anarchists.[19] The ministry informed Gueshov in Constantinople, Shopov in Salonika, and Standchev in St. Petersburg that absolutely no proof existed to place the brigands in Bulgaria, and it assured them that the government was taking stern measures to prevent the band from crossing the border, including the dispatch of additional soldiers to the border patrol.[20] Nevertheless, wrong impressions continued to plague the Bulgarian government.

Leishman, for example, stated his conviction that the brigands were in Bulgaria and that the Bulgarian government was not doing all it should to obtain Stone's release. He urged the State Department to send Dickinson to Sofia in his capacity as American agent to impress upon the Bulgarians the importance of the kidnapping in American eyes and the serious consequences of Bulgarian complicity, direct or indirect, in the affair.[21] Dickinson finally agreed to go to

Sofia, but his departure was delayed by Haskell's arrival in Constantinople on September 28 with the ransom demand.

Neither the American Board nor the State Department was willing to pay the ransom, for fear of setting a precedent.[22] Moreover, the department could not advance any sum without Congressional authorization. On October 3, A. Adee, the acting secretary of state, recommended in a telegram to Judson Smith, foreign secretary of the American Board, that the ransom be raised through private contributions. Adee formally assured Smith that the United States government would make every effort to secure the money from the government found responsible for the kidnapping, or, as a last resort, the administration would urge Congress to reimburse the contributors. On the basis of this highly specific set of assurances, a committee of Stone's friends and employees of the *Christian Herald* began raising the ransom through public subscription, but without participation of the American Board. The committee set up an account for contributions at Kidder, Peabody and Co., and Smith telegraphed the State Department on October 5 that the money could be raised.[23] The department, in turn, wired Eddy, the chargé d'affaires (Leishman left Constantinople for vacation on September 24), to make it clear that although the money would be raised, neither the United States government nor the American Board would assume responsibility for paying the ransom—"We simply do not obstruct charity."[24]

Although the American government encouraged the raising of the ransom, telegrams from the State Department to Eddy and Dickinson repeatedly stressed that the government was not to be involved in negotiating or paying the ransom, but it merely would give facilitative assistance. Discretion, the telegrams stated, was of the utmost importance in all dealings with the brigands, and all work was to be carried on with the full cooperation of the American Board treasurer, Peet. The "paramount interest of the United States is to save Stone."[25] Dickinson's instructions were very specific: "You are authorized and directed to exert yourself in your character as agent accredited to the Bulgarian government. You will keep in communication with the missionary treasurer, being however careful to abstain from discussing any question of responsibility and will not commit yourself or your government in that regard. You will do all in your official power and discretion to relieve the situation. You may go to Sofia if so doing will help the matter. You will observe strict reticence as to all you may do. You will render all assistance that is possible in trying to secure Miss Stone's release using utmost discretion."[26]

Dickinson arrived in Sofia on October 4. In the following months, he completely disregarded the State Department's instructions. He appointed himself official negotiator for the release of Stone and alienated the Bulgarian government, the Russian ambassador in Sofia, the American legation in Constantinople, most of the missionaries, and the Department of State. Immediately upon arriving in Sofia, Dickinson called at the Ministry of Foreign Affairs to present an American request for Bulgarian cooperation to secure Stone's safe release. Since the foreign minister, Danev, was out of town, Dickinson again called at the ministry on October 5, only to find that Danev was at his home. Dickinson went directly to Danev's house and demanded an interview, but Danev refused, saying that his house was undergoing repairs, and there was no appropriate room in which Dickinson could be received. Dickinson would not be put off; he insisted that the messages he brought from the United States government were extremely important and urgent, and he convinced Danev to agree to meet him next morning, Sunday, at the ministry.

Dickinson did indeed have a number of messages from Washington to relay to Danev. The State Department had received reports, not only from Dickinson but also from the Russian ambassador, Zinoviev, in Constantinople, that Stone's abduction was "without a doubt" the work of the Macedonian committee which was based in Sofia. Declaring that the United States attached "very great importance" to the safe release of Stone, Dickinson informed Danev of these allegations and said the United States "counted on" the powerful assistance of the Bulgarian government to effect Stone's release. As a first step, Dickinson suggested (on his own initiative), that the Bulgarian government hold all officers of the Macedonian Secret Committee (IMRO) living in the border regions responsible for the safety and release of Stone.[27]

Dickinson followed up his interview with Danev with a diplomatic note reiterating his suspicions of the Macedonian Secret Committee and adding that he believed the band was led by "Doncho of Dupnitsa." Dickinson had learned, he wrote, that Stone had been asked to contribute to the Macedonian cause in July, but she had refused. She had then been followed from the time she arrived in Samokov in July until her capture in Bansko. Following Washington's instructions, Dickinson stated, the "people of the United

States are thrilled with horror and indignation" over Stone's abduction. On his own initiative, he went on to urge the Bulgarians to take this unique opportunity to cement good relations with the United States by cooperating heartily, and to threaten that negligence in following up the involvement of the Macedonian committee would constitute an unfriendly act against the United States.[28]

The following day, October 8, Dickinson sent a second and even more strongly worded note to Danev on instructions from the State Department.[29] Noting that the kidnapping of Stone was the first such incident in American history, he said the president had asked him to say that "in view of converging evidence of complicity of Bulgarians" in the kidnapping, "if harm comes to Miss Stone, the American people will be satisfied with nothing less than unhesitating ascertainment of responsibility and due redress." Although this note did not specify actions the Bulgarian government should take, it lent great authority to Dickinson's previous demands that the Bulgarian government, against its will, hold members of the Macedonian committee responsible and use them to make contact with the kidnappers. At the same time, the note put the burden of proving themselves and their government innocent of any involvement on Bulgarian officials.

The State Department communicated to its representatives in St. Petersburg and Constantinople Dickinson's suspicions of the Bulgarian government and his attempts to force it to move actively against the kidnappers. The department had contacted Charlemagne Tower, its minister in St. Petersburg, almost immediately after receiving news of the ransom demand. In telgrams of October 3 and 5, the department instructed Tower to request the help of the Russian government and Russian diplomatic agents in Sofia and Constantinople in obtaining Stone's release. Another telegram asked Tower if the Russian agent in Sofia could be persuaded to intercede with members of the Macedonian committee on Stone's behalf. Tower met with Count Lamsdorff, the Russian Foreign Minister, on October 5. Lamsdorff expressed his sympathy for Stone and pledged Russian cooperation and help. Even before this meeting Lamsdorff had instructed Zinoviev, his minister in Constantinople, and N. Etter, the chargé d'affaires in Sofia, to exert their influence on Stone's behalf.[30] In addition, Lamsdorff summoned D. Stanchev to express his impatience with the Bulgarian government and his bafflement over why the Bulgarians were not acting as the American government had requested. He strongly recommended to Stanchev that it was in Bulgaria's interest to "move energetically" to save Stone's life because otherwise Bulgaria might lose European favor, and possibly America would take serious steps against her. Stanchev transmitted these unpleasant warnings to his government and asked to be informed of the concrete steps his government was taking in order to reassure Count Lamsdorff.[31]

Bombarded by the Americans, the Russians, the English, and the Turks with demands for "energetic measures" and with thinly veiled accusations of complicity, bad faith, and inaction, the Bulgarian government moved to the defensive. It seemed to Bulgarian officials that the Turks, the English, and the Americans were exploiting the kidnapping in order to compromise Bulgaria and discredit her in Europe. Their position was that the kidnapping did not take place in Bulgaria, and there was no hard proof of complicity of Macedonian Supreme Committee members. Moreover, the fact that Turkish troops could find no traces of the band in Turkey did not mean the band was in Bulgaria. There was, thus, no reason to hold Bulgaria responsible and no obligation on her part to negotiate for Stone's release.

The Bulgarians made clear this position to Dickinson, to the Ottoman commissioner in Sofia, to the American ministers in St. Petersburg and in Constantinople, and to Count Lamsdorff, among others. In addition, the Bulgarian government informed these diplomats of measures being taken to prevent the kidnappers from crossing the border and to track them down if they had slipped across unnoticed, including reinforcing all military posts near the border under new commanders; sending all peasants from the frontier to the interior to cut off food supplies to the brigands; increasing border guards; detaching large numbers of troops to Guel-tepe as Dickinson requested; searching mountain caves, forest huts and frontier villages for signs of the band; and watching some former supreme committee members who might be in communication with the band. In other words, they were doing everything that could possibly be done without more specific facts to work on and without transgressing the country's laws.[32]

Mikhail Sarafov, Minister of Internal Affairs, addressed a strong protest to Dickinson, detailing the measures the Bulgarian government had taken. Sarafov protested that despite these measures, Dickinson continued to accuse the government of not cooperating. The Bulgarian government had decided it could not allow a ransom to be paid on Bulgarian territory because "the many brigands which operate in a neighboring country" would "flock to Bulgaria where they could feel assured of receiving the ransom they demanded." As an example to others, the bandits who captured Stone would be caught, if possible, and punished without mercy. Sarafov concluded by saying that if the United States continued to insist on Bulgarian responsibility, Dickinson must turn over any information he had collected to the Bulgarian courts for action within the legal framework of the country.[33]

Sarafov's note seemed to make no impression on Dickinson. He never referred to it in his correspondence with the State Department, and it caused no modification in his behavior towards the Bulgarian government in the long run. Dickinson did note a temporary change in attitude on the part of Bulgarian officials from skepticism and indifference to one of concern and action, and attributed the change to the president's message. At one point, he even wrote that the Bulgarians were doing everything they "dare do or can do."[34]

This softening of Dickinson's attitude and his understanding of the problems the Bulgarian government faced in dealing with the Macedonian committee (if there were such problems) did not last long. Dickinson soon returned to the offensive with demands, accusations, and complaints. On October 11, he wrote to Danev, asking him to arrest two of the three muleteers who led Stone's travelling party, because he claimed to have proof that the two had prior knowledge of the kidnapping and were, therefore, partly responsible for it.[35] A few days later Dickinson applauded the arrest of five men in Dupnitsa who were thought to be members of the kidnapping band. But the Bulgarian government could not keep these men in jail on suspicion, and Dickinson refused to supply proof of their participation until after Stone's release. The Bulgarian government had no choice but to release the muleteers and the men in Dupnitsa, and Dickinson was furious that they did so without his consent. He persuaded Etter, the Russian chargé, to complain to Vernazza that the Bulgarian government was not cooperating. Supporting Dickinson's position, Etter personally urged action against persons suspected by Dickinson because of the seriousness of the affair.[36] This left the Bulgarians with a dilemma which was basically unresolvable—Dickinson would not share his "evidence," and they could not jail someone without it.

Dickinson's explanation for his refusal to reveal his sources was based on a single experience of James McGregor, the English chargé.[37] In late September, McGregor had told M. Sarafov about information

received from Asen X. Vasilev, a resident of Samokov, which impli-
cated IMRO in the kidnapping, and immediately afterwards, Vasilev
was arrested. Dickinson was sure that the Bulgarian government
would similarly arrest any source he named, thus intimidating his
contacts and shutting off information. He promised his sources ano-
nymity and kept his promise. Dickinson maintained he was not in
Bulgaria to aid the Bulgarian police department but "to collect and
report facts" for the sole use of his government. He insisted that the
police would find ample evidence of Macedonian committee participation and members' names if they inquired diligently in frontier
villages as Dickinson had done.[38]

*   *   *   *   *

Dickinson made no attempt to negotiate for Stone's release during his first few weeks in Sofia and, in fact, gave the impression that
he was not willing to pay a ransom. To be fair, Dickinson was not
officially authorized to pay Stone's ransom until late October. Therefore, in mid-October, with only a week remaining before the kidnap-
per's deadline, troubled by rumors that some of the brigands wanted
to kill the unransomed women and by the wintry mountain weather
which endangered them, Dickinson decided only a rescue attempt
would save them.

He had been told by a "confidential agent" on October 7 that the
band and its captives were in hiding at Guel-tepe (Vikhren in Bulgarian), the highest mountain peak in the Pirins on the Bulgarian-Turkish
border, near the village of Eleshnitsa. The band, described as composed of eighteen men (eleven Macedonians and seven Bulgarians),
supposedly had let it be known that it would surrender with the
women unharmed to Bulgarian soldiers, but would kill the women if
surrounded by Turkish troops. Dickinson was confident that all his
information was correct—it wasn't; the band was in Turkey and had
no intention of surrendering to anyone—and that the band would
surrender to Bulgarians "because no Bulgarian jury ever convicted
anyone involved in a crime done in the name of the Macedonian
cause."[39] He therefore concocted a plan: Bulgarian soldiers would
wait in ambush on the Bulgarian side of the mountain while Turkish
troops drove the band into the waiting net. Although he conferred
with the Russian chargé, Etter, Dickinson did not seek approval
from the State Department or notify Eddy in Constantinople. Instead, he immediately sought an appointment with Danev to get

Bulgarian cooperation. Finding Danev out, Dickinson insisted on seeing Vernazza and finally called on him about 11:00 P.M. on October 7. With Etter interpreting from English to French, Dickinson outlined his plan to Vernazza and suggested that the Bulgarian government send troops to surround the group, stationing them both on the Bulgarian side and, with permission, on Ottoman territory. Once the band was surrounded, two or three Bulgarian soldiers could be sent to negotiate for the band's surrender.[40]

Vernazza found this plan "strange." He told Dickinson that the Bulgarian government was not willing to negotiate with brigands under any circumstances, and besides, the Porte would never let Bulgarian soldiers onto Ottoman territory. Vernazza wondered, if the kidnappers were so willing to release their captives if surrounded, why could they not simply free them without pressure and without running the risk of being captured and imprisoned themselves. Dickinson did not explain his theory of Bulgarian justice to Vernazza but asked for a description of the terrain and an estimate of how long the government would need to deploy troops around the mountain peak.[41]

It is clear from Vernazza's notes of the conversation that he rejected all of the plan, except an increase in troop strength in the area, but Dickinson did not realize this. Possibly he thought the subsequent deployment of a company of soldiers to Peshtera (near Guel-tepe) signalled agreement with his plan. He seeemed to believe these soldiers were waiting for his signal to move against the band. On October 8 Dickinson sent a telegram to the State Department relaying the incorrect idea that the Bulgarian government was confident that it could arrest the kidnappers without endangering the lives of Stone and Tsilka.[42]

Having already put the plan into motion, Dickinson began to have second thoughts about the wisdom of moving troops, and asked the American minister in St. Petersburg, Tower, and the State Department for advice. The State Department had already received a number of telegrams from Eddy arguing vehemently against the plan and urgently recommending the withdrawal of Bulgarian troops from Guel-tepe. Eddy considered the plan foolhardy and was furious that Dickinson had not informed him ahead of time. Eddy notified the State Department that both the Bulgarian and the Russian ambassadors in Constantinople thought the plan unwarranted and dangerous, and demanded to know if the department was more interested in Stone's life or the kidnappers' punishment.[43]

On October 12, the State Department replied to Eddy and to Dickinson that the danger of Stone dying in such a rescue attempt was too great. The department would approve the plan only if the Bulgarian government could guarantee her safety, a condition that not even Dickinson would ask it to satisfy. The department suggested that instead of attempting Stone's rescue, it was better to hand over part of the collected ransom on "terms that will assure the deliverance of Stone." Count Lamsdorff supported the department, telling Tower in St. Petersburg that since the women were in Turkey, negotiations must begin immediately, or Turkish troops would surely kill them.[44] The problem with Lamsdorff's suggestion was that neither Dickinson nor the missionaries knew how to get in touch with the brigands. Haskell returned to Samokov on October 8, because Stone's letter said the money was to be delivered in Samokov.[45] But, perhaps because his house was being watched by Bulgarian authorities, he waited in vain for some word from the band.

In Sofia, Dickinson informed M. Sarafov of his intentions to enter into negotiations with the kidnappers to obtain Stone's release through payment of a ransom, and he requested Sarafov's help in getting in touch with the band. Sarafov declared that although the Bulgarian government could not be involved in such negotiations, it would not obstruct a humanitarian enterprise. Sarafov ordered the prefect of police to pick two men to act as Dickinson's emissaries to the band, and to supply them with documents that would allow them to travel unhindered through the frontier area. Since Dickinson did not feel he had the authority to send a specific ransom offer with these men, nor did he have enough time to consult with Eddy, he charged them simply with making contact with the brigands and reporting on the well-being of the women. He gave them letters for Stone and asked for her reply to prove she was well. The men left Sofia about October 22; one went to Nevrokop, the other to Gorna Dzhumaia.[46]

Dickinson confided to the Russian agent, Bakhmetiev (who had just returned to Sofia from St. Petersburg) his willingness to contact the band, but his inability to do so. Bakhmetiev offered to send a personal emissary, at his own expense, to get in touch with the band and set up an avenue for negotiations. Dickinson refused, according to Bakhmetiev, because "his instructions from Constantinople did not authorize him to promise any ransom, however small."[47] Bakhmetiev, certain that it would be impossible to save Stone without paying the ransom, decided to send an emissary anyway to see if she was still alive. He made arrangements with a well-known Sofia bookseller, K. T. Boyadzhiev, to send Lazar Tomov, then a student in Sofia (later a member of IMRO). Tomov agreed to try and find the band and left Sofia around October 25, carrying a letter for Stone from her former pupil, Kaseorova, a close friend of Bakhmetiev's wife.

Before Dickinson's or Bakhmetiev's emissaries had time to make contact with the kidnappers, an agent of theirs, probably Krüstio Asenov, approached Haskell.[48] On October 25, Asenov brought a second letter to Haskell from Stone, extending the time limit for payment of a ransom a final eight days. Armed with a power of attorney signed by Stone and Tsilka, Asenov was ready to collect the full sum. Haskell had no idea how much ransom money was available, but he was sure it did not amount to the full ransom demanded. He told Asenov that he was willing to discuss a lower ransom, and Asenov left Samokov to get permission to negotiate, promising to return shortly. As soon as Asenov left, Haskell notified Dickinson of the impending start of negotiations. Dickinson left Sofia for Samokov on October 29 to await the agent's return. His presence there was not welcomed by Eddy or Peet, who thought that Dickinson would probably spoil Haskell's work.[49]

Eddy and Peet suspected Dickinson's willingness to pay a ransom. As early as October 13, Dickinson had asked the State Department to stop revealing the amount of ransom money raised, as such news would increase the kidnappers' expectations and impede an early settlement. On October 26, the State Department informed Dickinson that $66,000 was available to pay a ransom (Haskell was told on October 30). Dickinson reasoned that if he offered such a large sum, the band would want even more; therefore on October 27, he asked permission to say that contributions had stopped and some monies had been withdrawn "on account of establishing a dangerous precedent." The State Department not only denied this request but also sharply reminded Dickinson that it was willing to pay a ransom, and he must work toward that end.

Dickinson did not have a chance to interfere with Haskell's negotiations because Asenov never returned. Dickinson attributed this to the publication in Constantinople newspapers of the start of negotiations.[50] It is also possible that Asenov, while passing through Dupnitsa on his way back from Samokov, learned of Lazar Tomov's arrival and decided it was not wise to go back to Haskell.

Tomov had given Kaseorava's letter for Stone to the regional IMRO chairman and suggested that someone accompany him back to Sofia to negotiate with Dickinson.[51] Asenov returned to the band on October 29. He asked Stone to write a note on the back of Kaseorova's letter. At the same time, Stone wrote a full account of their situation to Dickinson, stressing the inclement weather, the cold, and the thinness of their dresses. She begged him to do all in his power to free Tsilka and herself from their misery and assured him that she had much confidence in his ability to do so, not only because he represented the great and powerful United States, but also because he was a personal friend and a good Christian.[51] Stone also wrote a letter to her mother and brothers for Dickinson to mail. Asenov and Chernopeev brought these three letters and the power of attorney which Stone had signed in early October to Tomov, and returned with him to Sofia about October 31. Through Boyadzhiev, Tomov delievered the letters to Bakhmetiev, who got them to Dickinson when he returned from Samokov.

Dickinson waited three or four days in Samokov for the brigand agent to return; then he sent "a man believed to have planned the abduction" to negotiate with the brigands (probably Asen X. Vasilev). Dickinson impressed on this man the importance of the affair and the gravity of the consequences if anything happened to Stone, and he offered to pay 10,000 *lira* ($40,000) ransom. Dickinson expected prompt results from this man who was to make contact with the band and then report to him in Sofia.[53] When Dickinson returned to Sofia on November 5, he found that Bakhmetiev's emissary had located the band and had brought back an agent to negotiate with Dickinson. That evening, Asenov (without Chernopeev) came to Dickinson's room in the Hotel Bulgaria for the first time.

Dickinson held three meetings with members of the band: one with Asenov, one with Chernopeev, and one at which both Asenov and Chernopeev were present. Little is known about these meetings because neither Asenov nor Chernopeev mention them in their memoirs, and Dickinson reported little of their content to the State Department. Legend has it that Dickinson was very impressed with Asenov, but refused to deal with Chernopeev. According to Kharizanov, at their first meeting Dickinson told Asenov that he knew the members of the band were not highwaymen, but Macedonian revolutionaries, and he was sure they could come to some agreement. Unfortunately, he added, at this point there were "formal barriers put up by the Turkish government" which prevented him from negotiating.[54] Peyu Chernopeev claims that Dickinson refused, at this first meeting, to deal with the kidnappers, insisting on negotiating through the Bulgarian government. Asenov informed Dickinson that he and his compatriots had absolutely no connection with the government and, in fact, counted it as one of their enemies.[55] What really was said is unknown. The only thing we can be sure of is that Dickinson did not discuss a ransom offer with Asenov and that Asenov left the hotel furious at the way he had been treated.[56]

Dickinson's meeting with Chernopeev on November 8 also produced no concrete agreement. Chernopeev gave him a letter from Stone saying that she and Tsilka were healthy and that their "captors well know the need of keeping us as well as possible."[57] It was not until the third meeting on November 13 that Dickinson offered to pay 10,000 *lira* for Stone and Tsilka. This was much less than the band expected, and Asenov and Chernopeev left Sofia to confer with Sandansky.

These three meetings in early November were just the first steps towards an agreement between the band and Dickinson. Although Dickinson did not again meet personnally with Asenov and Chernopeev, he seems to have kept in touch with them through an unnamed intermediary.[58] Through this intermediary, Dickinson learned that the band was not willing to settle for 10,000 *lira* because they knew more was available. Dickinson made no counteroffer, and talks were stalemated for some time. During this period, Dickinson formulated an alternate plan for freeing the women. He had word that the women were hidden in Rila Monastery, guarded by only four men. Dickinson proposed to offer these four men a bribe (the money to come from the ransom fund) to let the women go, on the grounds that if the ransom were paid, the four guards would get none of it.[59]

Dickinson was not the only one with impractical ideas for rescuing the women. On November 10, Eddy asked permission from the State Department to send Gargiulo, the legation's translator, to Salonika because the British consul general there had contacts with an agent of the brigands who was willing to betray his comrades for a certain sum of money.[60] William Peet, who on October 6 had ruled out offering a reward for the delivery of the women, suggested on November 26 that a band of brigands be hired to steal Stone from her captors. Peet calculated that such a rescue would cost only 500 *lira* ($2,000).[61]

None of these plans were put into action, but the fact that they were even discussed shows that the Americans were impatient with the delays and anxious about the well-being of Stone and Tsilka. They had been captives for three months, and their release was not in sight. After consulting with Peet and Eddy, Dickinson issued an ultimatum to the brigands through his intermediary. He let it be known that his final offer was 10,000 *lira*, and if it was not accepted within a week's time, the money would be returned to the contributors, and Dickinson would abandon all attempts to come to an understanding with the kidnappers. In order to give more force to this ultimatum and to show that the Americans were full of confidence, Dickinson left Sofia for Constantinople, arriving there on November 26.[62]

Why did Dickinson delay reaching a settlement, and, with 14,500 *lira* at his disposal, why did he refuse to offer more than 10,000?

Dickinson felt himself on the defensive, conspired against by everyone, responding to complaints and inquiries about his inability to secure Stone's early release. From mid-October, he refused to confide in Bulgarian officials for fear that his information would be passed to the Macedonian Supreme Committee. Sure in his own mind that the supreme committee had planned the kidnapping, he was equally sure that the Bulgarian government would not act against the committee because the latter was not only "stronger than the government, in fact it is the government."[63]

Dickinson came to distrust Bakhmetiev and the Russian mission as well. He decided that the Russian government was using the Macedonian movement to make Ottoman rule intolerable in Macedonia and "thus destroy the Treaty of Berlin and give the Treaty of San Stefano validity and force."[64] He was convinced, as well, that public employees in Sofia and Constantinople, especially those in the telegraphic agencies, had "no secrets which are kept from the public," and that they freely gave away his dispatches.

But Dickinson laid most blame for his inability to reach an early agreement with the kidnappers on newspaper reports which, he complained, gave the brigands an exaggerated idea of their importance in American eyes and raised their expectations. He asserted that foreign and local newspapers published confidential information directed to him almost before he received it. As early as October 29, Dickinson protested to the State Department that he was being forced to consult too many people and could not do so without seeing a full account of these consultations appear in the daily press. The danger of leaks also made him most reluctant to share information with his colleague, Eddy, in Constantinople. They had no shared code service, and without one, it was "manifestly impossible for Eddy to advise me or for me to advise him . . . without giving the matter to the public." Dickinson was particularly incensed because shortly after he wired Eddy that he believed the band was hiding at Gueltepe and asked Eddy to enlist Ottoman military assistance in surrounding the area, this story had appeared in the press. This publicity, Dickinson was sure, had prompted the band to move to a different location shortly afterwards. In addition, the press had reported that the American legation had 100,000 *lira* ($400,000) at its disposal to ransom Stone. Dickinson claimed the kidnappers regarded such stories and the general lack of secrecy as "evidence of bad faith on our part" and as a way to "embarrass and delay negotiations."[65]

There seems some truth in Dickinson's assessment of the role of the press in hindering his negotiations, but his behavior towards the Bulgarian government and Bakhmetiev surely compounded his difficulties. He had begun dealing with the Bulgarian authorities with a series of sweeping, arrogant demands that were unlikely to bring cooperation. As the months wore on, he lied to them about matters which they doubtless were able to verify. For example, he told them he had had no direct contact with the kidnappers and that the missionaries in Samokov were the only Americans negotiating.[66] Yet it is most likely that the Bulgarian government knew of his meetings with Asenov and Chernopeev. Lack of confidence and ill-will thus mounted on both sides.

Dickinson entertained two contradictory impressions of the Bulgarian government and its role in the Stone affair, yet he never seems to have realized that they were contradictory. On one hand, he thought the Bulgarian authorities were doing everything possible to frustrate his negotiations with the band because it did not wish the ransom to be paid on Bulgarian soil; it preferred to deal with the brigands by military means even if this meant endangering Stone's life. On the other hand (as noted above), he was convinced that the Macedonian Supreme Committee controlled the Bulgarian government as well as the kidnap band, and this explained what he saw as Bulgarian inaction. Thus Dickinson complained of both "unwarrantable interference" and "extraordinary movements of scouting and search parties" as well as of indifference, lack of courage or vigor, and

only perfunctory moves to locate the bands and arrest the people
Dickinson suspected.[67] As an example of the latter attitude, he
cited the Bulgarian reaction to a diplomatic note he sent Danev,
stating that the band was hiding on Bulgarian territory in a village
called Bilirik, between the ravines of Grecheva and Christova; Danev
had replied that there was no such place and therefore Stone could
not be on Bulgarian territory.[68] As evidence of interference, Dickinson claimed that his emissaries (unnamed) were arrested, and his visi-
tors (also unnamed) detained for questioning. In a letter to the State
Department, he went so far as to say his mail was being opened and
read by the Bulgarian authorities.[69]

Although the State Department accepted Dickinson's mistrust of
the Bulgarian government, it did not share his view of Bakhmetiev or
the Russian government, and several times ordered Dickinson to "cooperate heartily" with Bakhmetiev because "his help is valuable."[70]
But instead of being grateful to Bakhmetiev or even acknowledging
the essential role he had played in arranging Dickinson's first meeting with Asenov, Dickinson suspected Bakhmetiev's intentions and
implied (to Washington) that his own agent in Samokov had done all
the work. In several telegrams to the State Department, Dickinson
asserted that since Bakhmetiev's return to Sofia, the Russian legation
was not cooperating as it had done before. Bakhmetiev, he claimed,
refused to help him get in touch with the band unless Dickinson was
prepared to pay the full 25,000 *lira* demanded. Dickinson also accused him of hating the Protestant missionaries and of asserting that
in the Stone kidnapping they had received their proper reward for
meddling in a place where they did not belong. Bakhmetiev, Dickinson said, sympathized with the Bulgarian government and, with his
support, the government could relax efforts to locate the band. He
thus refused to take Bakhmetiev into his confidence, although he
continued to consult with him, cautiously, and he would not tell
Bakhmetiev how much ransom money was available for fear that he
would tell his government or the Bulgarians.[71]

Dickinson's attitudes and feelings were not lost on Bakhmetiev.
On the same day that Dickinson telegraphed Washington to say he
was working "in harmony" with Bakhmetiev, the latter announced
that the Russian legation in Sofia would have nothing more to do
with the Stone affair.[72] Bakhmetiev told Dickinson that if and when
Dickinson was really interested in paying a ransom, he would have
no difficulty in contacting the band and securing Stone's release. If

harm came to Stone, Bakhmetiev warned, the responsibility would rest squarely on the shoulders of the person charged with ransoming her, who had not yet seriously attempted to do so. In describing this conversation with Dickinson to Vernazza, and in a telegram to Count Lamsdorff, Bakhmetiev erroneously accused Dickinson of having spent $8,000 of the $49,000 he had available in the unfruitful haggling process.[73]

The Bulgarians also objected strongly to Dickinson's behavior. They felt he had come to Bulgaria not with the intention of saving Stone, but rather to provoke and compromise the Bulgarian government. The position of the Bulgarian government was that while it would not object to negotiations being carried on in Sofia or in Samokov to secure Stone's release by ransom or other means, such negotiations were neither its business nor its responsibility. The task clearly was Dickinson's, but he compounded his own difficulties and then blamed the Bulgarians for his lack of success.[74]

In a long letter detailing the Bulgarian government's cooperation and castigating Dickinson's methods of operation, the Foreign Minister countered, for what he hoped was the last time, Dickinson's many complaints. Pointing out that the border had been strongly reinforced to prevent illegal crossings at Dickinson's own request, Danev asked how Dickinson could then expect persons without proper identification, such as Dickinson's agents, to travel freely through the area without being suspect. The Bulgarian government, he reminded Dickinson, was willing to make arrangements for Dickinson's emissaries, as the prefect of police had done earlier, but since Dickinson refused to reveal the names of his agents to obtain for them special travel passes, the Bulgarian government could not be blamed when these agents ran into trouble at the border. Nor, continued Danev, could Dickinson legitimately ask the Bulgarian government to suspend its laws and police measures in Sofia, Samokov or elsewhere to suit his convenience, or to arbitrarily jail citizens or others on the basis of Dickinson's suspicions. Danev concluded by stating that the negotiations were Dickinson's responsibility, not those of the Bulgarian government. If he had complaints, he should offer proof; without proof, there was no basis for governmental action.[75]

Danev followed up this letter to Dickinson with one to his minister in St. Petersburg, D. Stanchev. Bringing Stanchev up to date on the actions of the Bulgarian government and Dickinson's machinations, Danev noted that he had just received from Dickinson a copy of a new letter of credence designating him as diplomatic agent to Bulgaria, the letter which Prince Ferdinand had requested on October 16. Danev, citing Dickinson's "objectionable behavior" since his arrival in Sofia, felt he was clearly not the person who could best fulfill the aim of bettering U.S.-Bulgarian relations. He entrusted Stanchev with the task of tactfully relaying to his American colleague in St. Petersburg Bulgaria's objections to Dickinson, its desire for better relations, and the suggestion that the State Department would do well to appoint another person for the job.[76]

Chapter IV
Stone and Tsilka in Captivity

During the months of diplomatic activity, negotiations, and schemes for their rescue, Stone and Tsilka had continued their trek through Macedonia, supported by their belief in God, and fed and sheltered by Sandansky and his men.[1] They moved from one hut or sheepfold to another, sometimes in rain, sometimes in snow, but always at night, stealthily, and usually in single file. The band refused to tell the women about the status of negotiations or even world events. It was not until two months after McKinley's assassination that Stone learned of his death.[2] The band told what they considered fairy tales about the negotiations, and consequently, the two spent dreary days wondering why the process was taking so long and whether they had truly been abandoned by the outside world they longed to see.

They passed days of anxious waiting in windowless, airless huts, always dark and smoky. On many days the women were forced to sit cross-legged in a cramped corner of some hovel, not allowed to speak above a whisper for fear of being overheard by a passing shepherd. Utterly miserable, they longed for privacy and something to occupy themselves. Until her pen ran out of ink, Stone carefully underlined the Bible passages that gave them special comfort in order to find these more easily; every morning they read and reread these passages.

Stone said in letters to both her mother and to Dickinson: "Our captors well know the necessity of keeping us as well as possible, if they want to receive the ransom."[3] Indeed, the band did its best to keep the women comfortable and happy, both out of desire and need for the ransom and for fear that some harm might come to Tsilka and her unborn baby. At night, when the weather permitted and if travel was unnecessary, the band invited the women to join them while they passed the time with jokes, dances, songs, and games. The men would spread cloaks for the women to sit on and piled straw or branches in back of them to protect them from the wind. The men tried to provide grapes, apples, nuts, or whatever was available and, as the time of the baby's birth grew nearer they brought more nourishing foods for Tsilka. When she became despondent, they organized athletic games or other entertainments to divert her. Even so, there were days when no quantity of songs or dances could cheer up the women.

After a time the members of the band no longer refused to talk with Stone and Tsilka but welcomed their company. Stone took every opportunity to propagandize among them, with some success, she maintained. She told Bible stories to anyone who would listen and described for the men some of "God's truths." She tried to impress upon her "blasphemous" captors the necessity of "being right with God and right with men," and she related as examples the stories of Joseph, Joshua, and Daniel. Stone even transformed her sermon on Daniel into a little temperance lecture, for she had noticed that her captors were much addicted to alcohol and tobacco. In one case, she cornered one of the younger members of the band and told him the sad story of some of America's "first young men" who had been rejected for army service in Cuba because of their "tobacco-hearts, which cannot be trusted to bear the shocks of war." The young man, much to Stone's satisfaction, tried very hard after that to give up smoking and even began reading the Bible.

Stone was always willing to lend her Bible to anyone interested in reading it. At one point, according to Kharizanov, she made a deal with Asenov. If he would read a few passages which she had marked in the Bible, she would in return study some of the literature he considered sacred. Asenov supposedly gave her a book by Karl Kautsky which she tried to read, but it made absolutely no sense to her. The Bible, in turn, reinforced Asenov's impression that God was an old man who could not accomplish his job without man's help.

The prompt actions of Haskell and the widespread movement in the United States on behalf of Stone and Tsilka greatly impressed the band. Nonetheless, until late October, they kept up the posture that they would kill the women if a ransom was not received within a certain time. The letter Asenov brought to Haskell on October 25 announced the final extension. Stone had been forced to write the letter in a sheepfold, under the watchful eyes and drawn gun of Sandansky. With the arrival of Lazar Tomov and his message that negotiations could be carried out in Sofia with an American diplomat, the band stopped threatening to kill the women. Although the band was determined to collect the money which they knew had been raised in the United States for Stone, they realized, according to Stone, that it was futile to set a time limit when negotiating with diplomats.

Stone and Tsilka had heard rumors of Haskell's and Dickinson's activities on their behalf, but not until Asenov brought Kaseorova's letter did they have concrete proof that they had not been forgotten. With joy and gratitude, they read and reread the letter; and even translated it into Bulgarian for their captors. When they realized they would have to return the letter, they were heartbroken. Asenov suggested they copy it and then write a note on the back for Kaseorova. Pen and paper were brought and the "precious words" copied and laid carefully inside the Bible for safekeeping. Stone and Tsilka filled a delightful day with writing first the reply to Kaseorova, then a plea to Dickinson, and finally a letter of reassurance to Stone's mother.

At the end of October, when Asenov and Chernopeev started for Sofia, they left a much happier group of captors and captives. The men were satisfied, now that negotiations had started in earnest, that they would soon receive their money. The women felt reassured that their pitiful state was known to the outside world and that their friends were not standing idle. But the days dragged on without word. Tsilka became terribly depressed. Her baby was due soon, and she could prepare nothing for its arrival. Stone took it upon herself to inform their captors that preparations must be made, and after a long argument they grudgingly allowed her to make a list of essential items.

When the package arrived, Stone and Tsilka tore off the wrapping in their eagerness to begin work. Instead of soft flannel, they found coarse white homespun that the men used for leggings, and instead of cotton a type of cheesecloth used to clean guns. But the women did not mind; Tsilka optimistically observed that the wool would soften with washing, and from it she cut several blankets to protect the baby from the cold and one little shirt. From the cheesecloth, she managed to make three dresses, two hats, and two tiny shirts, plus kerchiefs for herself and for Stone. Time, which had hung so heavy before, now sped by with work. To prolong the work, the women used very fine stitches and by the time they finished, no baby had a finer wardrobe. They bound the blankets with cotton and embroidered them and filled the dresses and shirts with tucks and decorative stitching.

There had been no word from Asenov or Chernopeev for weeks, even though Stone was sure that Dickinson would arrange a settlement before Thanksgiving. The day before Thanksgiving Stone felt terribly homesick and despondent and spent all day pacing back and forth in the tiny hut. Tsilka explained to one of the guards who commented on Stone's unhappiness that the next day was an American holiday on which friends and family always gathered to celebrate God's generosity. The next morning, to their great surprise and utter delight, one of the brigands approached them as they were rising and nonchalantly said a turkey had been killed, how would they like it prepared. The day was a combination of Thanksgiving and Christmas for the women, because with the turkey came a bundle of warm woolen socks and thick woolen long underwear to protect them from the bitter cold.

No one told Stone or Tsilka that Asenov had brought these presents on his return from Sofia. They did not want to spoil the holiday atmosphere with Asenov's news that negotiations had failed and Dickinson had returned to Constantinople. Out of consideration for the women, Asenov did not appear until the next day. With a stern face he told the women the depressing news. He informed them also that money had been raised in the United States for their ransom and the band was determined to keep them, for five years if necessary, until they received that money. As if to prove their determination, Asenov said the band would take the women to a spot where no one could ever find them.

Stone and Tsilka could do nothing in the face of such determination except plead for warmer clothes to wear on the journey. The men doubted that the women would be able to sew dresses by hand, but they complied with the request, supplying thick, brown homespun wool and even thicker white homespun, along with huge needles, strong thread, and thimbles. Someone even remembered to bring buttons and decorative braid. Warned that they had to hurry, the women struggled with the unwieldy cloth, cutting and stitching with stiff and bruised hands. Within two days they completed the clothes.

Dressed in their homemade creations, which looked like something between a dress and a sack, the women began a new trek through the snow-covered mountains. Buffeted by piercing winds and bitter cold, they clung to their horses, climbing even higher than before. They finally arrived at a clearing in a forest where there were two newly built huts. The band planned to spend the winter in this spot, which was about two hours from a village called Sushitsa. The women's cabin, the smaller of the two, had just enough room for a fireplace and a rough bed on the floor. The brigands' cabin, although larger, had no fireplace and barely enough room for all the men to lie down. These huts had been so hastily constructed that large chinks between the split logs let in blasts of cold air. Although members of the band gave the women their cloaks to keep warm, it was impossible to stay warm in the cabin. So for the first time since their capture, because this spot was considered sufficiently isolated, the women were allowed out during the day to sit with the men around a blazing fire built in the middle of the clearing.

This hiding place did not turn out to be as safe as the band expected. Four or five days after they had settled in, a letter from Sava Mikhailov (who was still teaching in Gorna Dzhumaia) warned that a supreme committee band led by a local bandit, Doncho, was heading toward Sushitsa, intent on stealing the women. Doncho was offering 20 *lira*, a Mannlicher rifle, and a Nagant revolver to anyone who would join him, and his band was growing rapidly. Chernopeev and Asenov left immediately with six of the band for nearby Leshko to organize a "militia" to repulse Doncho's attack. On their way, they learned that Doncho was headed for the village of Troskovo, and sent a special messager to Sandansky. But Sandasky had already bundled the women onto their horses, and was headed for Troskovo.

Sandansky was forced to stop against his will when Tsilka suffered terrible pains and could go no further. In a house on the outskirts of Troskovo, the band shoved the women into a closet while Sandansky and his six men stood watch around the house. Cowering in their dark hole, the women prayed for salvation and agreed that "if worst came to worst, we would take our death at the hands of the guard that stood over us, rather than fall into the hands of these unknown highwaymen or of Turkish troops." Fortunately they did not have to make that choice.

Shortly after dark, a burst of rifle fire showed Sandansky that Doncho and his men surrounded the house. After a short exchange of fire came dead silence. Sandansky waited until dawn and then decided that Doncho had been scared off for some reason, and it was safe to move the women farther away from the village. The men hurried the women to the waiting horses, but a shot fired just as Tsilka was being mounted forced a hasty retreat back into the closet. Once again, they waited anxiously. At one point, a young man arrived to say that the coast was clear and they could leave the house, but the band, suspecting treachery, shot him.

Sandansky, desperately afraid that the gunfire had attracted the attention of Turkish patrols, resolved to make another escape attempt. This time, they did not allow the women to ride but cautiously led them on foot up the steep hill in back of the house. The expected shooting did not materialize, and they successfully gained the top of the mountain, where the women hastily mounted, not caring that the horses were not saddled. Shortly afterwards, Asenov and Chernopeev met them with a group of forty men. They had driven off Doncho's band by attacking it from the rear. Captors and captives alike greatly rejoiced in their escape, but they also feared that Doncho might attack again or that Turkish patrols would invade the area. Sandansky resolved to take the women to Bulgaria, while Asenov was sent to Sofia to see if there was any progress towards a settlement.[4]

Sandansky and the women crossed the border for the second time through Frolosh and headed once more for the village of Tservishte. The women were confined day and night in one room. While Tsilka hoped the baby would be born quickly so she could have something to take her mind off their interminable captivity, Stone dreaded the birth, fearing complications during delivery, the brigands' reaction to a crying baby that would attract attention, and the dangerous cold. Many times she pleaded with them to release Tsilka before the fateful day. But the men seemed to think that a settlement was imminent, and they procrastinated. On December 17, the men announced to Stone that they were prepared to take whatever sum had been raised in the United States and be content with it.[5] They ordered her to write a power of attorney for the money. Differing from the last power of attorney which said the bearer was authorized to collect the full ransom demand, this one declared the bearer able "to receive the ransom demanded for us, but with added powers to treat the question of our ransom to its final conclusion."

Sandansky had planned to take the women to his native village, Vlakhi, where he could assure Tsilka more comfortable surroundings when she gave birth. The house to house searches by the Bulgarian government in the area of Kiustendil and Dupnitsa accelerated Sandansky's plan. He moved the women into a new hiding place one day before the soldiers searched the house they had occupied. As soon as the soldiers were out of the village, Sandansky left with the women for Turkey. They arrived in Pokrovnik, near Gorna Dzhumaia, on December 21 and left immediately for Vlakhi. For ten days the group travelled an average of eight hours a night over rocky and steep paths.

Tsilka, weakened by ever stronger labor pains, suffered terribly during this journey, and many times refused to go on, insisting she would rather die on the spot. At one point, when it was impossible to continue on horseback, Tsilka would not dismount and had to be lifted off her horse and carried by one of the men, who continually whispered reassurances in an attempt to comfort her. When it became clear that Tsilka could not travel any longer, the group stopped at an isolated hut used by a wine-grower. The small hut was dominated by two huge wine casks, one old and broken, but the other brimming with fresh wine. They lit a fire and carefully arranged straw-and-leaf beds for the women. One of the men suggested they sleep well because the group would have to travel the next day. Stone informed him firmly that travel was impossible and pushed him out of the hut.

Late in the afternoon, Stone woke up to find Tsilka tossing and turning. She ordered all the men out of the cabin and demanded a kettle and a gourd for drinking. Towards dusk, an old lady appeared in the hut, evidently brought by the men from a nearby village. Ragged and dirty, she knew only the superstitious customs of her mountain village. Nonetheless, she was the first woman Stone and Tsilka had seen for four months, and her solid appearance and her experience as a mother comforted the women. The old lady even made Tsilka laugh in spite of her pains by offering to sprinkle her with holy water and then demanded she blow very hard into a little tin box the woman had brought with her. Tsilka declined politely and put the old lady in charge of heating water, saying she would call her when the time came. Stone huddled by the fire through this whole ordeal, pale and terribly nervous, inquiring every so often if there was something she could do to help, although she had no idea what to do. There was nothing anyone could do to help Tsilka, and no medicines to ease her pain. Racked by labor pains and a terrible feeling of loneliness and despair, Tsilka asked Stone to give her rings to her husband if anything should happen to her; she then grasped the rings of the full wine cask and gritted her teeth.

The cries of a new-born baby filling its lungs brought the guard to the door of the hut.[6] With a look of relief, he asked shyly if it was a boy or a girl. Disappointed when told a girl, he nonetheless filled a gourd with wine for the men to toast the baby's health. Shortly after, Sandansky came into the hut. As he stood in the center of the room, gruff and embarrassed and not quite sure what to do, Stone put the baby into his arms. Slowly his whole demeanor changed. His face brightened, his voice became more melodious and his actions gentler. Afraid that the baby would catch cold, he brought her near the fire to warm her feet. Sandansky asked Tsilka for a list of essential foods, handed back the baby, and promised to return as soon as he gave the orders for procuring the necessary items. True to his word, he came back with barley for a hot gruel and promises of prunes, sugar, and tea.

Tsilka, exhausted from her ordeal, lay on the straw bed, fighting off sleep to keep watch on Sandansky, who was rocking the baby by the fire. It was a losing battle, and she awoke the next morning to find him still cradling the baby, but fast asleep. Touched by that picture of a huge, bearded man with revolver and dagger at his side, tenderly holding her baby, Tsilka felt comforted and reassured that the men would not harm her daughter.

Towards evening, Sandansky asked if the rest of the band could pay customary respects to mother and daughter. Tsilka agreed and wrapped the baby in her finest blanket. One by one the men entered the cabin. Looking their best, their hands and faces cleaner than ever before and their weapons glistening, each congratulated the mother and blessed the baby, then shook hands with the old village woman and Stone. As each man went through this hastily assembled receiving line, he squeezed over to make room for others. When they finished, there were two rows of roughly dressed, heavily armed men with smiling faces and dancing eyes. It was an unbelievable scene: the baby and wine gourd passed from hand to hand, the men laughed, joked, and bragged of the presents they would make for the baby. One offered mocassins, another a whistle, a third said he would sew a brigand's outfit for this daughter of the band. There was no question of captors and captives that night but a gathering of friends and brothers. The men rejoiced that their fears had proved groundless, and Stone and Tsilka thanked God for the tremendous transformation in these men they had thought cruel and heartless. Elena Tsilka, or Kesmetchka (the lucky one), was finally returned to her mother. The band filed out of the hut and took up their guard duties because the area was not safe. There had been no decrease in Turkish patrol activity, and the band was afraid of being discovered. They gave Tsilka one night to recover from her ordeal and then announced it was time to travel.

Tsilka was still very weak and could not sit up for more than a few minutes at a time. Sandansky gave orders to build a box which would be strapped to the horse for Tsilka to ride in. All day long,

PLATE I

Left to right: Sava Mixhailov, Yane Sandansky, Krŭstio Asenov.

PLATE II

Ellen Stone

PLATE III

Katerina Tsilka and baby Elena (from *McClure's Magazine*)

PLATE IV. *Yane Sandansky's band in late 1902 or early 1903. Sandansky, center, with full beard.*

PLATE V. *Xhristo Chernopeev's Band in 1903. Chernopeev seated in middle of front row, with thin dark mustache.*

PLATE VI. *Typical Macedonian Band, circa 1903.*

PLATE VII. A typical Balkan town of the turn of the century.

PLATE VIII. *A typical Balkan town of the turn of the century.*

the sounds of hammering reached the two women. As the time approached to leave, the old midwife hung a piece of string around the baby's neck with a silver coin and a piece of garlic on it to ward off evil spirits. She then wrapped the baby in so many layers of cotton and wool that it looked less like a baby than a rectangular package of cloth. Next to the baby's skin she placed one of the cheesecloth shirts and a heavy cotton diaper; then a layer of cotton flannel, wrapped all around her and woolen flannel around her feet; on top of this she wound several woolen blankets, topped off by a very thick big blanket. She placed four sugar cubes near the baby's mouth to give her something to suck on and to prevent her from crying.

But the group did not travel that night. The box made for Tsilka weighed so much that none of the horses could bear the load. A great argument ensued as to whether Tsilka should remain behind with one of the men, both of them dressed as peasants to fool the patrols if they should pass. Tsilka refused to remain by herself with her daughter, and Stone refused to travel without Tsilka. Surprisingly, several members of the band supported the women and declared they were prepared to remain behind with the women and fight if discovered.

Tsilka unwrapped the baby and settled back on her straw pallet for the night. The next day, they built a lighter box and found a stronger horse. The man who was to carry the baby came in to practice holding her. To Tsilka's suggestion that if he was to carry the baby, he ought to give his gun to someone else, he replied that he would be defenseless without his gun and would not dream of giving it up. Tsilka was very uneasy about letting one of the men carry Elena because she feared that if the baby cried at the wrong time, he would kill her. Stone offered to carry Elena; she donned a sling-like contraption which went over her shoulder and around her waist, leaving her hands free to hold on to the saddle. With the baby wrapped and in the sling all that remained was to settle Tsilka in her box.

Tsilka regarded the coffin-like box as a symbol of her coming death, and she cried hysterically when strapped into it. Four men lifted the box and tied it to the crude saddle. On the other side of the saddle they tied a motley assortment of luggage and logs to balance the weight, but the box immediately slid back until it almost touched the ground. The horse, without any encouragement, moved so quickly up the steep, narrow path that the men could not control it, nor could they support the box to make Tsilka's ride more comfortable. The box banged on rocks, hit trees, dragged along the ground

with poor Tsilka so tortured and frightened, she could not even cry.
At one point, the band had to madly scramble to keep the box from
upsetting at an especially steep spot and spilling Tsilka down the hill.
At other times, only with groups of men pushing on both the box
and the balancing logs could the horse make it up the hill.

The trip was no easier for Stone, who had to keep one hand firmly around the baby, while holding on desperately with the other to
the swaying saddle. Sometimes, she had to be supported by the men
as she tried to find the sugar cubes which had been tucked into the
baby's wrappings. At other times, the men had to support her to
keep her from falling backwards off the horse at particularly steep
places. The trip seemed endless, over some of the worst terrain they
had ever encountered. On the occasions that everyone was commanded to absolute silence, Stone worried that the baby would cry
and give them away. Tsilka became hysterical about midway in the
journey because she could hear the baby crying, but the men would
not stop so she could nurse her. With superhuman effort, Tsilka
broke the straps which bound her, as she struggled to sit up and
make her demand heard.

After eight hours of agony, the weary group arrived in or near the
village of Vlakhi. The hut was much like all the others, with boarded-
up windows, no chimney, and a smoky wood fire. The baby had survived the journey very well, except for a "disordered stomach"
which was cured by castor oil. Tsilka had suffered much more, but
after a few days of rest she recovered some of her strength.

The group continued to travel frequently, but the journeys were
never longer than two hours. Although the snow blew and the wind
roared, the men always found a sheltered spot for Tsilka to nurse,
and the travel was easier to bear. Stone and Tsilka were much comforted by the thought that their days of captivity were almost over.
They filled their time caring for Elena, unaware of the diplomatic
obstacles still to be overcome before they would be released.

Chapter V
Final Diplomatic Efforts

Reports that Tsilka had died during childbirth and Stone had died shortly after from grief were widespread during December. Although the diplomats and missionaries in the area did not put much faith in these particular reports, they despaired of the women being released alive.[1] They blamed Dickinson for this state of affairs, accusing him of mismanaging and bungling the negotiations in Sofia. In an internal memorandum, an official in the State Department noted that Dickinson had "wasted time and aroused distrust and resentment by trying to make out a case against the Bulgarian government instead of working solely to secure Miss Stone's release."[2] The feeling in Constantinople, Eddy reported, was that the full sum of 25,000 *lira* would have to be paid, since the band was convinced that the legation had that much money or could easily raise it. Although Eddy was not pleased with the thought of paying so much, it seemed to him dangerous to haggle over the sum as Dickinson had done. Since the State Department had abandoned its original refusal to pay a ransom, the amount made little difference. It would do no more harm to pay the full 25,000 *lira* than the 14,500 Dickinson had offered. This was, after all, just a "pecuniary consideration which is unworthy of a great power which has the means of forcing a reimbursement."[3]

George Washburn, president of Roberts College in Constantinople, supported Eddy. Reporting on his trip to Bulgaria, Washburn stated that "there is no hope for [Stone's] release except by making terms with the brigands and paying a ransom," and that it was useless to pursue negotiations in Bulgaria, as neither Stone nor the band was there. Washburn recommended that the legation send a "trusty person who knows the language and the people" to the Salonika area to open negotiations.[4] Building on Washburn's recommendation, Eddy asked the State Department for permission to send Gargiulo and Peet to Macedonia with a "final offer" of $66,000 (15,000 *lira*). If they could not get the brigands to accept this sum, the United

States government had three options, all "extreme measures." It could either "1) pay the full 25,000; 2) request that the Turks and the Bulgarians use troops to capture the band; or 3) coerce the Bulgarian government into being responsible for Stone's release, possibly by sending warships to Varna."[5]

The State Department was unwilling to suggest raising more money in the United States, nor did it seriously consider any of Eddy's ideas for "extremist coercive measures." Instead, the department supported the creation of a negotiating committee, and suggested that if the committee had difficulty contacting the band or getting a settlement, they could always break off negotiations and let the brigands make a move.[6] To ensure the negotiating committee's success, Eddy publicized the news that $66,000 was all that was available for a ransom. He called in Gueshov on December 18 to enlist the Bulgarian government's help in spreading the story. Even though Gueshov thought the affair none of his business, Eddy insisted Gueshov read a telegram from the State Department authorizing Eddy to pay $66,000, and asked Gueshov to relay the information to his government.[7]

Peet and Gargiulo, two of the three members of the negotiating committee, left Constantinople on December 17 for Salonika. They intended to go to Gorna Dzhumaia or the Razlog district, where they would make known their desire to negotiate and where they hoped an agent of the band would contact them. They had already decided to ask Dr. John House to accompany them as translator. The legation gave these three full responsibility to deal with the kidnappers, even though they were to refer to themselves as agents of the American Board. The polite fiction was that they were not on a diplomatic assignment but were friends of Stone's who were ransoming her with the kind help—advice, instructions, and facilitation of movement—of the legation. Leishman, who had returned to Constantinople on December 27, 1901, was not interested in the details of their negotiations and trusted them to come to an agreement satisfactory to the United States government.[8]

Upon their arrival in Salonika, about December 18, Peet and Gargiulo immediately set about makng contact with the band. They asked Shopov to find them a guide who knew the Razlog area well and could help them get in touch with the band. Shopov declined, saying it was impossible to find such a person in Salonika and he, therefore, could be of little help.[9] Through Biliotti, the British consul, Peet and Gargiulo engaged and dispatched on December 22 a messenger, who was to offer 14,000 *lira* ($61,000) and bring back proof of Stone and Tsilka's well-being. On December 23, Peet, Gargiulo, and House left for Serres to await an answer. At the same time, Peet wrote an unnamed acquaintance in Sofia, asking him to publicize the fact that he and Gargiulo were prepared to negotiate and pay 14,000 *lira*. They waited some time, encouraged only by the fact that Biliotti's messenger seemed "to have communicated with leading figures of the movement." Based on this flimsy hope of establishing contact, Gargiulo and Peet reported their "partial success" to Eddy on December 26; Eddy, in turn passed the news to the State Department that Peet and Gargiulo were "in close touch with the brigands."[10]

Negotiations for Stone's release took place in two parts: one concerned the ransom amount and the second the time and place for the exchange of money and release of the women. Negotiations about the ransom amount were the subject of much misunderstanding and the source of great conflict between Dickinson on the one hand, and Gargiulo, Peet, Leishman and the State Department on the other. In appointing a negotiating committee, Eddy assumed that only its members would treat all questions pertaining to Stone's release. As far as the legation was concerned, that excluded Dickinson. Dickinson had failed when he had the chance, and now the legattion regarded his help and suggestions as interference. In an attempt to curb Dickinson's activities and put him more fully under the legation's control, the State Department ordered Dickinson to send all his communications relating to the Stone affair through the legation, rather than directly from the consulate.[11]

From the time Peet and Gargiulo left for Salonika, the legation ignored and refused to take seriously Dickinson's information, and they rejected his attempts to negotiate. While Leishman at first did not require Dickinson to break off his relations with his "agent" in Sofia, he refused to let Dickinson resume negotiations through him.[12] Later, first Eddy and then Leishman reminded Dickinson a number of times that negotiations were no longer his business. But Dickinson was never directly instructed by the State Department to refrain from negotiating, and he never ceased to consider himself, and by extension, his agent, as the authorized and official represenatives of the United States government to the kidnappers.

In reply to Leishman's categorical statement that Dickinson's agent had no authority to negotiate, Dickinson asserted that the authority conferred on himself "has never been withdrawn or modified, but on the contrary has been repeatedly recognized by the

department, and it follows . . . that while in Bulgaria, I had at least
coordinate power with the legation and that any agent I empowered
to treat with the brigands would have as full authority to act in Bulgaria as anyone the Legation might send to the Turkish frontier."
According to Dickinson, this authority came from the State Department's instructions of October 26 to Eddy to honor Dickinson's
draft for the ransom money and from Eddy's authorization to Dickinson to begin ransom talks by offering as low a sum as possible.[13]

This misunderstanding between Leishman and Dickinson degener-
ated into an argument over which agents were really in contact with
the band and which were simply dupes of "alleged confederates"
like the one Dickinson had "wasted money on in his first days in
Sofia." Dickinson warned Leishman that Peet and Gargiulo were
probably "being imposed upon by one or more of the alleged confederates of the region who will undertake for a consideration to put
anyone in communication with the brigands," but could never do
so.[14] Leishman, in turn, accused Dickinson's agent of providing
"vague and unofficial" information upon which it was impossible to
base any concrete actions. Moreover, Leishman suspected that Dickinson's agent was not negotiating with an authentic representative of
the band, but with someone who had no right to act in its name.[15]
Gargiulo and Peet got into the argument by saying Dickinson was deliberately undermining their chances for success by allowing his
agent to offer 500 *lira* (about $2,000) more than they offered. Fur-
thermore, Gargiulo falsely accused Dickinson of sabotaging negotiations by writing to people in Sofia that there was more money available.[16]

Even though Peet and Gargiulo daily expected word from their
agent, it was Dickinson's intermediary who secured an agreement
with the band. As early as December 24, the agent, probably D.
Todorov, a former student of Dr. House—House is the only one to
mention Todorov by name—reported to Dickinson that the band was
willing to settle for less money than previously demanded. What persuaded the band to change its mind is not clear, but in any case
Dickinson believed Todorov and asked Leishman for permission to
go to Sofia to resume negotiations. Leishman refused to let him go,
adding in his telegram to the State Department that Dickinson's
presence in Sofia would just complicate matters.[17] Dickinson then
instructed Todorov to notify the brigands of Peet and Gargiulo's
arrival in Salonika and their ability to pay the full amount raised as

ransom. The fact that there were now, in effect, two sets of negotiators in the field gave the band the possibility of receiving the money either in Turkey or Bulgaria, whichever was more convenient.

Whether this information was communicated to Asenov is not clear. Stone says in her memoirs that her captors dealt only with Dickinson's agent and with Dr. House (whom they thought answered to Dickinson), and they did not learn of Peet and Gargiulo's existence until the middle of January. This is supported by Dickinson's statement that Asenov offered to work out details with James Baird, a missionary, in Samokov (Bulgaria) or with House in Bansko (Turkey), but Asenov never mentioned Peet and Gargiulo.[18] About January 1, after Dickinson had told Todorov exactly how much money was available, Todorov and Asenov reached a firm agreement. Asenov agreed to accept 14,500 *lira* ($63,800) and to discuss terms of exchange in Bansko with Dr. House.

Dickinson had kept Leishman posted on these developments right up until he reported agreement on the ransom figure. But Leishman refused to take this agreement seriously because he considered Dickinson's agent an unofficial meddler in affairs assigned to the negotiating committee, and probably also because Dickinson had cried wolf too often. Instead of following up on Dickinson's agreement, Leishman told Dickinson to take no action except to impress upon his intermediary that "he had no authority for the present to enter into negotiations."[19]

Dickinson either paid no attention to Leishman's order or misunderstood it. He came away from his interview with Leishman on January 1 convinced that Leishman had agreed with Dickinson's plan to send House to Bansko to make preliminary arrangements. Dickinson suggested the exchange should take place near or at a railway station to avoid the need for a conspicuous guard for the money. Dickinson would go to Plovdiv to be able to authenticate Stone's endorsement and be ready to pay a ransom in Bulgaria, if that was necessary, while Leishman directed the activities in Bansko.[20] After his interview, but without full consultation with Leishman, Dickinson wrote a personal letter to House asking him to go to Bansko where the kidnappers would seek him out to discuss the place and conditions of payment and release, which must be simultaneous, Dickinson insisted, in accordance with legation policy. The kidnappers would identify themselves with a note from Dickinson's agent endorsed by Stone.[21]

On January 3, Edward Haskell, the missionary in Samokov who had received the original ransom note, delivered a letter from Todorov to House in Serres, repeating the contents of Dickinson's earlier letters and promising that House would receive from the kidnappers in Bansko another copy of Todorov's letter with Stone's endorsement. House showed the letter to Peet and Gargiulo and asked their permission to go by himself to Bansko. Peet and Gargiulo did not really believe that an agreement had been reached, perhaps because of the absence of Stone's signature on the letter Haskell brought. They were not pleased with the idea of letting House go without them and were annoyed that they had not been consulted by Dickinson before such arrangements were made. Gargiulo thought it strange that the message should be specifically directed to House when the negotiating committee included three people. Peet assumed that House had been in on the old negotiations and was, therefore, known to the brigands. Leishman, when he heard of Dickinson's request to House, was furious and again ordered Dickinson to take no further action.[22] In the end, they agreed to let House go, with the understanding that he would arrange a meeting at which Peet and Gargiulo would discuss terms. With this understanding, House left Serres for Bansko on January 6, ostensibly to do missionary work.[23]

On January 12, Asenov returned to the band, which was hiding in the village of Vlakhi, with news of his agreement on the ransom amount and his upcoming meeting in Bansko with House. He brought with him a copy of Todorov's letter to House, which he asked Tsilka and Stone to endorse in such a manner that House could be sure there was no forgery or trickery involved and which would authenticate the bearers as her captors.[24] It was decided that Asenov, Sandansky, and Sava Mikhailov would go to Bansko to meet House, while Chernopeev remained with the women.[25] Convinced that her kidnappers would release Tsilka and herself only after they received the money, Stone volunteered to write House, appealing to him to trust her captors and absolving him of all responsibility should the brigands fail to keep their word. With this appeal and the letter from Todorov, Sandansky, Asenov, and Mikhailov set out for Bansko about January 13.

House had been in Bansko since January 8, lodging with a local Protestant, Ivan Grechanov.[26] For a week, he carried out his missionary duties, meeting with local Protesants, holding church services and Bible readings. He had expected to be contacted immediately upon his arrival in Bansko, and the delay was puzzling. For Leishman, the fact that no one had contacted House just proved his suspicions of Dickinson's "agent." On January 6 and again on January 10, Leishman wrote the State Department about the lack of material progress. He was pessimistic about whether Stone was still alive and still waited for someone to contact Peet and Gargiulo with "confirmatory evidence" of her well-being. Dickinson's report that the brigands had left for Bansko, according to his agent, did nothing to set Leishman's mind at ease.[27] Peet and Gargiulo, in the meantime, having no luck in Serres, went to Gorna Dzhumaia on January 14 to be closer to House in case he received a message. They were accompanied to Gorna Dzhumaia by an escort imposed on them by the Ottoman authorities.

Finally, on the night of January 16 or 17, three fully armed men appeared at Grechanov's house in Bansko with Stone's letter. Although House was willing to conclude an agreement with Sandansky, Asenov, and Mikhailov, he did not have the right to do so without first consulting Peet and Gargiulo. House agreed in principle to hand over the money secretly in unmarked coins on January 25 at Kresenko Gorge near Bansko, and, in return, the women would be freed shortly therafter at a different location. The band agreed to return on January 22 to work out final details after House consulted with Peet and Gargiulo.

Asenov, Sandansky, and Mikhailov were surprised that House was not able to conclude an agreement on his own authority and left unsatisfied with the outcome, feeling not much closer to a resolution than before. Having assumed that they were negotiating through House with Dickinson, the three were greatly disturbed to learn that the agreement of Peet and Gargiulo—of whom they had not heard before—was also necessary. It is not surprising that they suspected bad faith. They returned to the band with a newsy letter from House to Stone which promised "I will endeavor to persuade the men who hold the money to come to the proposals of the brigands."[28]

The brigands were not the only ones upset by the outcome of this meeting with House. Stone and Tsilka were angry and perplexed at this sudden thwarting of their release by men of whose involvement they had never before known. Forced to write a "last letter," Stone pleaded with House to accept the brigands' conditions. Otherwise, they threatened to keep Tsilka and herself until the full 25,000 *lira* was collected and paid. Stone accused "friends" of prolonging their captivity and expressed complete confidence that their captors would try to fulfill every and any pledge they made.

After an indignant addition by Tsilka who begged for her daughter, Stone concluded that "no one had a right to hold back the money that had been given so long ago. . . . Our captors are exasperated with these repeated delays in the negotiations, and they enjoin upon us to write you not to expect another letter from us, if you do not now finish the work of obtaining our freedom."[29]

This letter, although justified in its sentiments, was actually unnecessary. Peet and Gargiulo had already dropped their demand of simultaneous exchange. Having been instructed by Leishman to "use their judgment and lose no time in making the best terms possible," Peet and Gargiulo, in conference with House who went to Gorna Dzhumaia on January 18, accepted the brigands' conditions that payment precede release.[30] Gargiulo cabled Leishman that Stone and Tsilka's expression of confidence, contained in the appeal delivered to House, led the negotiating committee to agree to payment of the ransom near Bansko and release of the women within ten days of the payment. All details had been worked out according to Gargiulo, except the place of delivery of the women.[31]

Shortly afterwards, Gargiulo cabled that the money should be sent through Serres to Demir Hissar (today called Sidiokastron, located about twenty kilometers from Serres on the main road to Bulgaria) by train, and from Demir Hissar to Gorna Dzhumaia by caravan. Gargiulo would arrange for a guard and horses to meet the party and suggested they spend the first night at Demir Hissar. In the same cable, Gargiulo insisted that Leishman secure, through the Ottoman Foreign Ministry, orders to all civil and military authorities not to interfere with the movements of the negotiating committee and to halt the guard where the committee requested. He demanded absolute secrecy for the negotiating committee's movements and plans.[32]

Leishman arranged for the Ottoman Bank in Constantinople to deliver to the Oriental Railway Station 15,000 *lira* ($66,000), to be placed in a special wagon which would be detached in Demir Hissar and routed to a place chosen by the negotiating committee. On January 20, the party accompanying the money left Constantinople: W. Smith-Lyte, a United States marshal, charged with handing the money over to Peet and Gargiulo; Lemmi, the legation's second translator, who would arrange details along the way; two bodyguards from the legation; two Croats from the Ottoman Bank; and six Turkish soldiers.[33]

Leishman, with much effort, secured the grand vizier's promise that the Ottoman government would: 1) halt all troop movements in the Gorna Dzhumaia area while negotiations proceeded; 2) order the guard escorting the money to halt and remain where requested by Gargiulo; 3) interpose no obstacles to the negotiating committee's meetings with the kidnappers; and 4) make no attempt to surround the place chosen for the exchange of the ransom money. In return, the American government would absolve the Porte of responsibility for any harm inflicted on the members of the negotiating committee by the brigands as a result of Ottoman cooperation. On January 23, Leishman received a diplomatic note from Foreign Minister Tewfik assuring him that the grand vizier had ordered the ministries of War and Interior to conform to Leishman's demands and to immediately instruct civil and military authorities in the Salonika area accordingly.[34]

The Ottoman government and local Ottoman officials cooperated fully with the legation and the negotiating committee, until it became obvious that the Americans intended to pay the ransom on Turkish territory. Although Leishman received assurance after assurance from the Porte and the Foreign Minister, their orders seemed to have no influence on local authorities who blatantly hindered the committee's attempt to meet the band and pay the ransom, and who tried to use the committee to discover and capture the kidnappers.

The Turks' delaying tactics and increased troop movements began with the arrival of the money at Demir Hissar on the night of January 21; the escort which was supposed to take the money to Gorna Dzhumaia at daybreak on January 22 failed to arrive. Lemmi and Leishman could do nothing to hurry the escort because it took twenty hours for Lemmi's telegram to reach Leishman. Not until the morning of the 23rd did the caravan composed of the United States marshal, Lemmi, a Turkish captain, twenty cavalry men, and three military guides set off in three carriages for Gorna Dzhumaia. About two hours after starting, the carriage carrying the money broke down and had to be abandoned. Requisitioning two extra horses, the caravan started again. All along the journey, they picked up soldiers; by the time they arrived in Gorna Dzhumaia on January 24, over a hundred soldiers guarded the money.[35]

As the negotiating committee continued its journey to Bansko with the money, difficulties with local Turkish authorities increased. While some officials acknowledged receiving orders to halt the troops and not interfere with the negotiating committee's movements, they claimed in the same breath to have orders from the Porte to prevent payment of a ransom in Turkey. Other officials interpreted their instructions to mean that troop activity should cease on the frontier but not in the interior. The provincial military commander at Serres, for example, secured an order that his troops should act if an attempt to pay the ransom in Turkey was made. Minister Tewfik vigorously denied this order and instructed the Serres commander to allow the committee and money to proceed to Bansko as planned. However, instead of taking Peet and Gargiulo to Bansko, the Turks escorted them to Razlog, and by the time they got to Bansko on January 26, the day after the money was to be handed over, 250 troops surrounded the village and blockaded all approaches to it.

Peet and Gargiulo settled in the Protestant Center while House remained with Ivan Gerchanov. The three men were sure that the brigands' agents had fled at the sight of so many soldiers, and they despaired of accomplishing their task with the troops watching their every move. They had no way of contacting the band, and were unable to prove they were sincerely interested in paying a ransom and were not acting in bad faith, as the delays and presence of troops suggested. By January 27, they were ready to give up and return to Serres in the hope of reopening negotiations there.

Meanwhile, Leishman actively campaigned with the Porte on behalf of the negotiating committee. From January 21 to 31, he petitioned the Foreign Minister almost daily to comply with his four requests. He reiterated in each interview and in each letter the full responsibility of the Porte to allow negotiations to continue and the danger that local interference might cause negotiations to fail. The strongest-worded warning was in a message of January 28: "The moral responsibility of preventing the payment of the ransom of Miss Stone by acts of the regularly appointed officers of the government is even greater than the legal and technical liability for her abduction, and I fear, will lead to more serious consequences . . . and is sure to cause the most unfavorable feeling throughout the civilized world." [36]

As a result of his efforts and threats, Leishman was able to reassure the negotiating committee of Turkish cooperation and suggested they remain a few more days in Bansko. A January 27 cable from Leishman especially encouraged the committee; it said that the district military commander "is and has been imperatively ordered by an *Irade* of the Sultan to put himself and his troops absolutely at your service and to do whatever you demand and not to do whatever you wish not done."

Typcially, it took almost two days for this order to reach the district commander. When it did, he refused to withdraw his troops from Bansko until Gargiulo furnished him with a declaration that no claim would be made on the Ottoman government for the ransom paid. Gargiulo certainly had no authority to make such a declaration, and Leishman had agreed to no such condition, nor did he intend to. Once again, Gargiulo cabled Leishman, demanding he remonstrate with the Porte; once again the Foreign Minister reiterated his government's sincere desire to cooperate, and on January 30, he ordered the district commander to comply with the *Irade*, with no conditions attached; Gargiulo, Peet, and House decided to spend one more night in Bansko.

That night, an agent of the kidnappers brought news that on the next day, January 31, they would dine at Konstantin Petkanchin's (the man to whom Stone had first written) with Sandansky, Asenov, and Mikhailov.[38] At this meeting, all agreed that to keep the payment secret, the gold should be replaced with lead, and the bank valises shipped back to Constantinople as if the place of payment had been changed. On February 1, Gargiulo cabled Leishman: "Matter going very satisfactorily. . . . Send Lemmi and two bodyguards to Drama to receive the valises and carry them back." And on the 2nd, Gargiulo cabled: "The ransom is paid to brigands' chief recommended by Miss Stone."[39]

How did the negotiating committee replace 230 pounds of gold with an equal amount of lead without being detected when, as House says, there were two sets of guards at the Protestant Center and a bevy of interested journalists all around?[40]

There are any number of explanations for how the money was transferred, but unfortunately few were written by the participants in the actual transfer. Gargiulo and Peet mention nothing at all about the exchange in their reports. House sums it up in three sentences: They bought the lead in the village and brought it in bags to Peet's room, "opposite the Turkish general's, in spite of the fact that the house was guarded by two sets of soldiers, one at the door, and the other at the gate. At last the gold lay unguarded in saddlebags under my bed at the other end of the village." This task was accomplished, House said, while the British journalists were dining with the Turks.

Sandansky says only that he suggested to Peet, House, and Gargiulo that they remove the gold and replace it with lead, but he offers no clue as to how the three men were to accomplish that task.[41]

Most of the explanations offered by later writers hinge on a fire that broke out at the main inn in Bansko where the district military commander and most of the soldiers and correspondents were staying. Thus Kharizanov claims that under cover of the "accidental" fire, House, Peet, and Gargiulo brought the lead to the Protestant Center and carried the gold out in their pockets during two or three hours of continuous trips back and forth between the Center and Gerchanov's house. Another author agrees with Kharizanov that the negotiating committee, under cover of the fire, carried the lead in and the gold out in their pockets. But he says that it took the committee all day of February 2 (not February 1) to get the lead from a certain Georgi Kolchagov's house to the living room of the Center, and the gold from there to Gerchanov's. Anton Strashimirov, in his biography of Krüstio Asenov, says that because of the fire, the three-man committee, two villagers, and the "village idiot" (Krüstio Asenov in disguise) were able to carry the bags of lead into the cellar of the Center where they exchanged the lead for the gold.[42]

The major problem with all these stories is that the fire broke out not on February 1, but a few days previously, although the exact date is not known. William Maud, a correspondent for the London magazine, *The Daily Graphic*, reported on February 22 that the fire at the inn occurred the same day that Peet and Gargiulo arrived in Bansko, January 26. Moreover, according to Maud, a court in Salonika later judged the fire accidental, although many thought it was set by IMRO.[43] House says that the fire broke out on a Thursday (January 30), the day he heard from the brigand's agent. Neither Peet nor Gargiulo mention anything about a fire, and it would seem reasonable that they should had it been instrumental in the exchange. In any case, they could not have used the fire of January 26 or 30 as a cover because they had as yet received no word from the band on the ransom arrangements.

Peyü Chernopeev postulates two other explanations for how the money was exchanged without the knowledge of the Turks. He assumes the exchange took place in the cellar of the Protestant Center and says it was possible either because Gargiulo ordered the guard withdrawn (as was his right by the Sultan's *Irade*) or because there was a secret underground passage to the cellar.[44] While the latter suggestion is most unlikely—the passage would surely have been mentioned by others if it existed—the former explanation may have some validity. But difficulties remain unexplained: 1) Gargiulo never mentioned using his power, and he complained about troop movements and lack of cooperation right up until the ransom was paid; 2) the authorities would certainly have suspected something was afoot after such an order, yet they were completely fooled by the return of the bank valises and had no idea the ransom was paid until two weeks after the fact; and 3) there were still many eager journalists trailing Peet, Gargiulo, and House, and they also never suspected the exchange had taken place.

It seems most likely that because the exchange had been so long delayed, the Turks and journalists had relaxed their guard, and no one noticed any unusual activity on February 1.[45] In fact, House attributed part of their success to the fact that he and his two colleagues had made it a habit since arriving in Bansko to take long walks through the village "for exercise," even though the weather was bitter cold; eventually, he said, the journalists gave up following them.[46] Possibly (but not likely, since it probably would have been found out and mentioned), the negotiating committee bribed the guards to look the other way while they carried sacks of lead and gold in and out of the Center. But in that case, it was strange that no one in the village had noticed three men lugging eighty-pound sacks from one end of the village to the other.

While we are unlikely to know exactly what took place with any certainty, it seems most likely that on February 1, House, Peet, and Gargiulo strolled back and forth between the Protestant Center and Ivan Gerchanov's. Each carrying about ten pounds in pockets or briefcases, they transported lead to Peet's room and gold to Gerchanov's house in eight trips. They then resealed the bank valises so skillfully that three British correspondents later said they "could swear that the bags had not been tampered with."[47]

That night, the money was taken from Gerchanov's house in saddlebags to a designated spot outside of Bansko, where it was handed over to Sandansky, Asenov, Mikhailov, and twelve other fully-armed men. In return, the negotiating committee received the receipt written on December 17, 1901, by Stone and Tsilka. The committee gave the kidnappers a letter for Stone which explained that they had resolved much earlier to trust the brigands' agents and accept their terms but had "met with difficulties from the government, which we scarcely overcame after several days of endeavor." The three relied upon the "word of honor" of Stone's captors to release her soon and would wait for her in Serres.[48]

Sandansky, Mikhailov, and Asenov went first to Plovdiv, where they left 2,000 *lira* with Mikhail Boyadzhiev, a local high school teacher. By train, they continued to Sofia, where they argued with Georcho Petrov and Toshe Deliivanov over where to hide the money and how to divide it up. They finally agreed to distribute the money among trustworthy friends, to be held until Gotse Delchev returned to Sofia from his tour of western Macedonia. They gave 4,000 *lira* to Krŭstio Asenov's sister; another 4,000 to Dimo Khadzhidimov, and the final 4,000 to a certain Uzunov, a telegraph operator in Sofia. Later the money was resdistributed in smaller sums: Anton Strashimirov guarded 300 *lira*, while part of the money held by Dimo Khadzhidimov was divided among fellow students of Asenov.[49]

Delchev returned to Sofia about March 10. At a meeting shortly thereafter, Sandansky, Delchev, Chernopeev, Asenov, and others elected Georcho Petrov, N. Maleshevsky, Toshe Deliivanov, and Sava Mikhailov to decide the best use for the money.[50] The committee decided to give 150 *lira* to the local revolutionary organization in Gorna Dzhumaia as compensation for any suffering or injury its members' might have sustained at the hands of Turkish authorities because the kidnapping occurred in their district. They gave a new revolver to each member of the band that kidnapped Stone and Tsilka. Although Chernoppev and Sandansky refused to accept any of the money they had worked so hard to collect, without their knowledge Gotse Delchev sent five *lira* apiece to Chernopeev's wife and to Sandansky's father. Delchev allegedly also gave 250 *lira* to Dime Mecheto, an anarchist, which he used to finance the Salonika *attentat* in April, 1903, during which a French boat and the Ottoman bank were dynamited.[51]

The rest of the money was assigned to buy weapons for an uprising that IMRO had set for the spring of 1903. The district of Bitola got 7,000 *lira*, and Razlog and Dzhumaia 2,000 apiece.[52] For some reason the Serres district received no money, and when the uprising did take place, only 150 Mannlichers were available there. In the districts that received part of the ransom money, preparations for the uprising were meager. Especially in the border regions, much to everyone's dismay, most of the money went to rout rival supreme commitee bands which were usurping IMRO's adherents throughout Macedonia. Only in Bitola did enough money remain to fight the

Turks. Thus during the Ilinden uprising in 1903, IMRO could strongly resist the Turkish soldiers only in the Bitola region.

In order to bring about Stone's release, the negotiating committee had to agree to certain conditions which later caused great conflict between House and the American legation, and between the American legation and the Porte. Peet and Gargiulo claimed that House had accepted these conditions, set at the January 31 meeting, without their knowledge. Gargiulo said House had tried to prevent his and Peet's attendance at this meeting. When they insisted on being present, House ignored them and held a long conversation with the brigands which he refused to translate.[53] House had accepted certain demands in the name of the United States government, for he considered himself an agent of the government as an official member of the negotiating committee, empowered by the United States legation. He felt it completely within his power to make promises on behalf of the United States and considered the kidnappers' terms reasonable. House agreed that the United States government would: 1) keep the place and time of exchange strictly secret; 2) do all possible to protect the innocent from Ottoman attempts to punish the kidnappers and not push the Ottoman government to molest, punish, or take vengeance on people who had innocently come into contact with the band; 3) make the same efforts to protect Tsilka as they did Stone from petty persecution by Ottoman officials; and 4) protect Konstantin Petkanchin and Ivan Gerchanov from being punished because of the help they had given the negotiating committee.[54]

When Leishman heard of these promises, he repudiated all but the first. While agreeing to keep the proceedings of the committee secret, he felt he could not agree to the other conditions which interfered with the internal affairs of Turkey. Leishman thought House had acted with "ulterior motives, merely using Miss Stone as a means to accomplish other purposes." He insisted that House had absolutely no right to make promises in the name of the United States government, and accused House of embarrassing him and the government. The negotiating committee to which House belonged had no official standing according to the American government, Leishman reminded House, and consequently, the word of the committee (and House) would not be considered binding on the government.[55]

Leishman did agree, very reluctantly, to one other concession the committee as a group had made: the cessation of all unnecessary troop movements for a ten-day period in the districts of Serres,

Demir Hissar, Uskup (Skopje), Melnik, Salonika, Nevrokop, Gorna Dzhumaia, and Razlog. Leishman objected because he feared such a "blanket" demand would never be met by the Turks but rather would arouse their suspicions and make them increase troop movements. In fact, repeated requests for compliance did sorely try relations between the Porte and the legation and its representatives.

Both Biliotti and Shopov reported from Salonika that there was much friction between the Americans and the Turks. Biliotti claimed that Gargiulo had threatened a blockade by the American fleet if the Turks did not cooperate, while Shopov said the negotiating committee had spent the whole time in Gorna Dzhumaia and Razlog arguing with the Turks. There was indeed friction between Gargiulo and the local Turkish authorities. Although the Porte had issued the requested orders, most went unheeded by zealous local officials, who did not want to be blamed later for failing to capture the brigands. Gargiulo, as before, insisted that instead of decreasing activity as requested, local officials had actually increased patrols. His appeals to the *Mutessarif* (mayor) of Serres were ignored. The latter, instead, accused Gargiulo of demanding absolutely no troop movement in the whole district of Serres while "negotiations" were being carried on.[56]

On February 2, Peet and Gargiulo left Bansko with the "unopened" bank valises. In Drama, they handed them over to Lemmi who headed for Constantinople, while Peet and Gargiulo went to Serres. Rumors abounded that negotiations had failed completely, and there was no possibility of their reopening. Leishman assured Gueshov on February 3 that these rumors were false, and that it was just a question of putting the final touches on an agreement. Leishman blamed the extraordinary movement of Turkish troops for the delay and said the committee had deemed it necessary to change its plans somewhat and adopt new methods. To ensure the success of these new methods, Leishman made the "unusual and stringent demand on the Turkish government" to cease troop movements as the committee requested.[58] In actuality, while portraying these demands as necessary for the conclusion of the ransom negotiation, Leishman was trying to set the stage for the easier delivery of Stone and Tsilka by the band. To ensure their release would not be aborted by a fear of capture by Turkish troops, he had to convince the Porte that the ransom negotiation was continuing. Thus the Turks would believe they might have later opportunities for capture. The Turkish government had difficulty understanding the logic of the legation's request, since the talks supposedly had failed and there was no sign of them starting again. Supporting the Turkish position were rumors that if the talks did reopen, they would be in Bulgaria and not in Turkey. For a few days, the government issued the requested orders, but by February 9, Leishmann noticed the "indifference" and hard-heartedness of the Foreign Minister which he could not counter without revealing that the ransom had been paid. Leishman's double game was becoming more difficult.

When the ten-day period allotted for the release of Stone had passed, neither sign nor word came from the kidnappers. Gargiulo suspected that increased military activity caused the delay. To get fuller Turkish cooperation, he, Peet, and House agreed that Leishman should inform the Porte that the ransom had been paid. Leishman consented and informed the Foreign Minister in a diplomatic note on February 12.[59] On the 13th, Gargiulo advised Lemmi, who had not yet reached Constantinople because of a break in rail service, to "get rid of his burden" and return to Constantinople via Salonika.

Strangely enough, no one wanted to believe the ransom had really been paid. Most thought the announcement just a ploy to detract attention while payment took place elsewhere. The Turks continued to dog the tracks of members of the negotiating committee and of Lemmi, even after Lemmi had gotten rid of the bank valises. Shopov noted that the Serres military commander "does not allow the Americans to take one step unaccompanied by an officer of his headquarters."[60] The Turks stepped up searches for the kidnappers and even besieged a number of towns around Demir Hissar in the hopes of capturing the band.

Under the constant pressure from Leishman in Constantinople and Gargiulo in Serres, the Ottoman government became very defensive. The commander of the 9th Military Division in Serres accused Gargiulo, again, of demanding "that all military movements in the Vilayet be stopped and that even the patrols which always make their rounds in the neighborhood of Serres, cease everywhere to circulate."[61] This would allow complete liberty to the "bands of Bulgarian brigands" to infiltrate and stir up trouble. In fact, according to the Foreign Minister, reports from Serres already showed increased activity by Bulgarian bands in that area.

The Ottoman position was that it was absolutely impossible to suspend the maintenance of order and security in the whole county of Serres, much less elsewhere, especially with the increased infiltration of bands. It was irrelevant that neither Gargiulo nor Leishman had made no such demand but had requested no "unusual" troop activities. The Foreign Minister still maintained that the delay in releasing Stone was a deliberate maneuver by the band to take advantage of the lack of patrols to infiltrate agents. If Gargiulo could furnish precise information as to where and when Stone was to be released, then and only then would the Ottoman government immediately clear the specified area of troops. But Gargiulo had no idea where the band was and could not be so specific.

It seems, in retrospect, that Gargiulo's insistence on the cessation of activities in such a large number of counties was a mistake, as Leishman had feared, and did cause a delay in the women's release by exciting the suspicions of the Turks. The Turks, on the other hand, seem to have deliberately misinterpreted and enlarged the request in order to avoid obeying it. The Ottoman government and, more particularly, local officials were bent on capturing the brigands—an act they considered would help them escape responsibility for the kidnapping and repayment of the ransom. The Foreign Minister tried a number of times to convince Leishman that Turkish compliance with American requests abrogated Turkish responsibility for the affair. Leishman refused again and again to accept this hypothesis, and the Turks, while paying lip-service to American requests in Constantinople, ignored them locally.

The long delay in releasing the women led Leishman to conclude the kidnappers had acted in bad faith and to formulate drastic measures to capture and punish them. He set two deadlines for the women's release (after the original ten days were up), the first was February 20, the second, March 1. At that time, he warned Gargiulo, he would notify Bulgaria and Turkey of his desire to track down the band. All promises of secrecy on the part of the negotiating committee would be annulled, and all known participants in the affair be put under surveillance.[62]

Both times Gargiulo managed to convince Leishman to be patient. While the band might be acting in bad faith, more likely they suspected the negotiating committee of bad faith because of the frenzied troop movements. Although Gargiulo still had no word from the band, he had sent out a number of messengers and had asked Dickinson's agent in Sofia for advice. Gargiulo suggested that Peet be sent to Sofia to learn something of the band's whereabouts. In all his dispatches, Gargiulo maintained his faith in the band's pledges and worried that the Turkish soldiers would surround the band and prevent the release of the women. On February 22, Gargiulo reported he had word that on February 20 a man had appeared in Bansko to say the women were well, and the delay in their release was due to the extraordinary activity of the troops. The next day, February 23, Biliotti wired Gargiulo that the women had been freed near Strumitsa (in the southeast corner of present-day Yugoslavia). After cabling Leishman the good news, Gargiulo, House, and the English journalist, Maud, left for Strumitsa to meet Stone and Tsilka and escort them back to Salonika.

It was indeed the activity of Turkish troops that caused the delay of three weeks between the ransom payment and release of the captives. Chernopeev decided to avoid the troops by heading north instead of south to Serres, as agreed upon.[63] From their hiding place in Vlakhi, he led the women due north through Oshtava and Senekos. A deep fog shrouding the mountains made travel extremely dangerous and delayed the travelers for several days. Turning northwest, they crossed the Struma River, heading for the village of Leshko. From there, they traversed the mountains which now divide Bulgaria and Yugoslavia and headed south.

The journey was as difficult as ever, and the danger of encountering Turkish patrols seemed even greater than before. Some nights the band refused to travel at all, much to the women's dismay. At one point Chernopeev explained to Stone and Tsilka that Turkish troops were very close, so close on five or six occasions that the band had despaired of freeing the women alive. On Stone's suggestion, the band sent a messenger to assure the Americans that she and Tsilka were fine and would soon be freed.

At the village of Razlovtsi, Chernopeev left the group and returned north to fight a supreme committee band. Under Andon Kuoseto, the group continued south for several days more. At last, in a dilapidated hut, high in the mountains, three men arrived to announce that Stone and Tsilka were to be freed that night. Very formally, the men told the women they could keep the clothes they had made during their captivity, and each would be given a goat's-hair cloak and a pillow for her pack-saddle. The men explained that after much discussion they had decided to give the women one *lira* for travelling expenses. In addition to the money, the men gave them some bread which Stone and Tsilka stowed in their saddlebags along with their original clothes and the baby's things.

The women mounted their horses and for the last time set out with their guards—one in front, one in back, and the rest at their sides. After about two hours, the women realized there were only two men left, the rest having silently disappeared along the way. For over six hours, the two women and two guards continued down through the mountains. About 4 A.M., the guards stopped and told the women to dismount. The men unloaded the horses and settled the women under a pear tree. One of the men pointed out a village in the distance and said he was sure that in the morning a passerby from that village would find them and help them carry their saddle-bags and pillows. Taking the horses, the men vanished.

It took a while for Stone and Tsilka to realize they were really on their own and did not have to sit in the cold until ordered to move. Tsilka slung the heavy saddlebags over her shoulders, while Stone carried the baby; she could carry no more, having injured her knee during the last journey. Ferocious barking halted the women's advance, and they sat down once more to wait for morning. But Tsilka could not wait; with her hands full of stones to throw at the dogs, she left Stone and the baby and went to find help. Stone felt Tsilka had been gone for hours. She was freezing cold and frightened that the baby would get chilled. Tsilka eventually returned with an old man, a Moslem Albanian, who helped them carry their belongings to the first house in the village. Although they were warmly welcomed and plied with coffee, Stone and Tsilka were too anxious to get to Strumitsa, the closest town, and refused to stay long. Their hosts took them to the village mayor who provided the women with horses and escorted them to Strumitsa.

They made as strange a procession as the one that began their odyssey. Two uncouth-looking women, their heads wrapped in white kerchiefs, their bodies hidden by the goat's-hair cloaks, escorted by a short, white-haired old man and an erect, strong young man wearing a white sheepskin coat flung over one shoulder. By the time the procession arrived in Strumitsa, it had been joined by crowds of curious onlookers, jostling to get a look at the famous captives. Stone and Tsilka went directly to the local Protestant mission and gratefully disappeared into the pastor's house. The local minister immediately sent a telegram to Salonika spreading the joyous news, while the women, for the first time in six months, luxuriated in a bath, clean clothes, and a hot, home-cooked meal.[64]

Chapter VI
Conclusion

Three separate problems had to be resolved after Stone and Tsilka's release. The first was to capture and punish their kidnappers; second, to determine governmental responsibility; and third, to repay those who had contributed the ransom money. Only the third problem was ever satisfactorily resolved.

Stone and Tsilka's captors revealed their identities only years after the incident. Until that self-revelation, no one was sure who they were. While the missionaries, the American officials, and the Turkish authorities were positive the kidnapping was the work of the secret Macedonian Committee, IMRO, they had no tangible evidence. As Leishman put it in a cable to the State Department, reports that the band was "composed wholly, or in part, of Bulgarian citizens and instigated and possibly directed by the Macedonian Committee, whose headquarters are at Sofia, are unsupported by testimony that would be of any real value, although I am morally certain that this is the case."[1] James Baird sent Leishman the names of fifteen men who, he said, had participated in the kidnapping. Only a few names on the list, which included the bandit, Doncho (who had tried unsuccessfully to steal the women from the band) were correct: Sandansky, the Prodanovi brothers, and four men from from Gradovo.[2]

The Turks' identification of band members proved even more inaccurate than Baird's. On March 31, an official announcement ran in the government newspaper, *Selyanik*, in Salonika, listing fourteen men whom the Ottoman government held responsible for the kidnapping. Neither Sandansky, Chernopeev, nor Asenov were on the list, which did include, as did Baird's, the Prodanovi brothers and four men from Gradovo and, unlike Baird's, a number of Protestants from Bansko.[3]

Contrary to expectations, neither Stone nor Tsilka were very helpful in providing information which could lead to the identification or apprehension of their captors. From the day of their arrival in Strumitsa until Stone's departure for the United States and Tsilka's return to Bansko, Ottoman authorities interviewed and questioned the women innumerable times. Their interrogation began immediately upon arrival in Strumitsa, with the local police commissioner spending "all day" asking questions. The next day, the mayor asked the same questions again because he was not satisfied with the police commissioner's notes. In Salonika, they talked to the *Vali*, the police chief, the military commissioner, the Bulgarian and British diplomatic agents, journalists, and American officials.[4]

In all these interviews, as in their articles in *McClure's Magazine*, Stone's and Tsilka's descriptions of their captors and their travels were vague and brief, filled more with anecdotes than facts.[5] Neither ever mentioned how many people composed the band, the names of the villages they stayed in, or the routes they travelled. Stone reported that the men, who were "unquestionably Turkish subjects," called each other by Turkish names and talked among themselves in Bulgarian, Turkish, Albanian, and Greek. All of them spoke Bulgarian to the women (Stone and Tsilka spoke only English and Bulgarian). Some of the men spoke a pure, literary Bulgarian, while others spoke a Macedonian dialect. Stone described the leader of the band (Sandansky) as an intelligent man, well-built, with a dyed moustache and beard. Even Stone's anecdotes provided little information. For example, she related an argument between the men one night as to the proper route to take. The argument, in Bulgarian, was won by a man who spoke pure, literary Bulgarian and evidently knew the area well. Not very much to base an arrest on.

While she probably told no outright lies, Stone "could not remember" much of the time. In one instance, the Bulgarian commercial agent, Shopov, asked her if, towards the end of their journey, they had crossed any large rivers (i.e., the Struma or the Strumitsa). Stone replied that she could not remember, yet this was only a week or so after she had waded across the Struma River on the trip from Vlakhi to Strumitsa.[6] The missionaries and American officials and, of course, the Ottoman government regarded suspiciously Stone's and Tsilka's reticence in providing details or descriptive information that could be used to capture the band. Tsilka and her husband, in particular, were suspected of having been party to the kidnapping. N. Shopov reported from Salonika that the circle around the American consul in Salonika believed that "Mr. and Mrs. Tsilka were aware of plans to capture Stone and the plan was carried out with their knowledge and agreement." Even Leishman suspected Grigor Tsilka, saying, "It was quite within the range of possibilities that Tsilka knew more or less what was going on."[7]

The Ottoman government, seeking to fob off legal responsibility for the kidnapping, supported wholeheartedly the idea of the Tsilkas'

complicity. The *Vali* in Salonika took this theory so far that he arrested Grigor Tsilka as an accomplice to the kidnapping, but was
forced to release him for want of evidence. Expanding on the idea,
the Ottoman commissioner in Sofia tried to convince Biliotti that
Stone and the American missionaries had planning the kidnapping as
a "pecuniary speculation."[8]

Most people did not judge Stone a willing participant in her own
kidnapping although many suspected her of not telling the whole
story. James Baird wrote House in early March that he was "suspici-
ous of Stone's inability to describe the brigands or the places they
had been." Edward Haskell seconded this view and sharply criticized
what he called Stone's refusal to cooperate fully with the Turkish
authorities. Leishman, although not blaming Stone, assumed that she
and Tsilka had taken a vow of secrecy under pressure from the
and were, therefore, not very helpful.[9]

Quite possibly, although Stone never mentions it, their captors
had threatened some type of retaliation if either she or Tsilka ever
revealed anything to the Ottoman authorities. Such a threat would
certainly intimidate Tsilka, whose family lived in Bansko, within
reach of IMRO. Stone, however, once she returned to the United
States, would be safe from any retaliation, and such a threat would
be ineffective. Perhaps she continued her silence to protect Tsilka's
family, or to preserve the interests of Protestant missions, as Shopov
and Gueshov suggested; perhaps, she deliberately protected her
captors.[10]

Stone did not reveal any more information about the band once
she returned to the United States, nor did she denounce her captors.
She may have given additional information in a book she was writing,
but the manuscript was destroyed in a fire at her home in Massachusetts in 1908. In fact, Stone became an ardent supporter of Macedonian independence and the leading exponent of Ottoman responsibility for the affair. In a series of lectures throughout the United
States in 1903 and 1904, Stone described Turkish atrocities in Macedonia and preached the necessity of freeing Macedonia from the
Ottoman Empire. She summarized the main thrust of her lectures at
the end of her memoirs in *McClure's Magazine*: "Had Turkey ever
fulfilled her promise, made twenty-four years ago in the Treaty of
Berlin, to introduce reforms for the betterment of the various Christian nations ruled over by her, Macedonia might not be overrun and
terrorized as now it is by brigands, and this strange spectacle of

women kidnapped by them and held in the heart of the Balkan peninsula for an exorbitant ransom might never have happened." She
wrote not a word against her captors.[1] Stone's lectures led many of
the missionaries to strongly censure her for "singing too much the
song of the brigands themselves." The American Board finally warned her that they would have to disassociate themselves from her if
she continued her anti-Turk, pro-Macedonian lectures.

As far as can be discovered, Tsilka never openly supported the
Macedonian cause, nor did she lay the blame for the kidnapping on
any particular group or country, although she did lecture in the
United States following her release on the political and economic
situation in Turkey. Her position, of course, was much more delicate
than Stone's because she was an Ottoman subject and suspected by
the government of complicity. As the brigands had assumed would
be the case, the American legation did not protect either Tsilka or
her husband, and they were subjected to unending questioning and
"petty persecution" for weeks after her release.[12]

Stone had not been particularly in favor of Macedonian independence before her kidnapping, or so Sandansky and Chernopeev
thought when they chose her as a target. Was she converted in captivity? Although she railed against her captors and accused them of
cruelty and heartlessness, she evidently trusted them. She preferred
to die with them than to fall into Turkish hands. She voluntarily
wrote to House, Peet, and Gargiulo, pleading with them to accept
the brigands' terms, and took all responsibility if the brigands refused
to release the women after receiving the ransom. Whether, as Kharizanov claimed, Stone was "well aware of the need to keep secret the
ideas and the participants in the affair" and to prevent their punishment and whether she really wrote two letters of thanks to Sandansky are irrelevant matters (and probably untrue).[13] She did, in any
case, support the "cause" in her own way after her release. It all
seems to suggest that Stone was indeed converted to, or at least convinced of, the righteousness of the Macedonian struggle by the sincerity of her captors.

There was great concern that the brigands' success in kidnapping
and ransoming Stone and Tsilka would encourage other attempts.
House, speaking for the missionaries, warned that unless "some
punishment is meted out," additional "outrages" were inevitable.
Leishman had mentioned the possibility in January that Congress
enact a bill after the women's release, authorizing $150,000 to be

used to capture the brigands as a deterrent to others. After the women's release, Leishman suggested to the Ottoman Foreign Minister that the Porte offer a suitable reward for information leading to the arrest and conviction of the kidnappers, but the Porte never acted.[14] The British government took the most sensible stance. In early March, 1902, it announced that it would not be responsible for any of its citizens, except government officials on official business, travelling through Macedonia.

The State Department instructed Leishman on March 4 to impress upon the Ottoman government the importance of redoubling its efforts to apprehend the brigands. Leishman made a number of such representations to the Porte and suggested that Dickinson urge similar efforts on the Bulgarian government. Leishman did not think anything would come of Dickinson's discussion with Bulgarian officials because of the difficulty of proving the complicity of Bulgarian citizens in the affair, but he thought something should be done for "moral effect." On March 18, under instructions from the State Department, Leishman directed Dickinson to address a note to the Bulgarian government stressing the importance of capturing and punishing the brigands, and protecting American rights to file a claim or make further representations at a later date. Leishman further recommended that Dickinson, at his "very earliest convenience," go to Sofia in order to make the representation in person.[15] Leishman had ordered Dickinson to represent American interests in Sofia only after confirming with him that the Bulgarian government had waived its objections to Dickinson's appointment, and that only formal recognition by Ferdinand was necessary to fully accredit him. Dickinson reassured Leishman that this was so on February 26.[16]

Dickinson refused to go to Sofia as Leishman sugggested because he thought the trip a futile one. Instead he offered to address the Bulgarian government through the mail or through Elliot, the British diplomatic agent in Sofia, whom Dickinson had asked to represent American interests while he was not in Sofia.[17] On March 26, the State Department ordered him to write a diplomatic note to Danev expressing American interest in the capture and punishment of the brigands, and he did so on April 5. The note went unanswered, but not because the Bulgarian government was disinterested in capturing the bandits. In fact, even before the women were released, the Bulgarian government had ordered "quick and strict measures on the border to prevent the brigands from escaping to Bulgaria or from sending the ransom money to Bulgaria."[18] Rather, Bulgarian officials had finally decided to openly declare Dickinson unacceptable to the Bulgarian government.[19]

A few days after Leishman instructed Dickinson to go to Sofia
and before Dickinson wrote to Danev, Gueshov showed Leishman a
telegram from Danev saying Dickinson would not be accredited as
the United States diplomatic agent in Sofia. Leishman asked Gueshov
to present his government's reasons for Dickinson's rejection in writing, which Gueshov did on March 28. Gueshov wrote that Dickinson
was unacceptable because: 1) Dickinson still maintained his position
in Constantinople in violation of the request made to him on August
18, 1901 (August 31 in the new calendar) and 2) Dickinson was
persona non grata to Prince Ferdinand on account of the attitude toward Bulgaria and the Bulgarian government which he expressed
while in Sofia during the autumn of 1901. The Bulgarian government would be pleased to accept someone else as diplomatic agent
in Sofia, but under the original condition that that person not be
accredited to Constantinople at the same time.[20]

Dickinson seemed to be unaware of the Bulgarian government's
position on his appointment to Sofia, and there is no evidence that
he received any orders to cease dealing with the Bulgarians. Leishman
did ask the State Department on March 29 whether he should counter-
mand previous instructions to Dickinson and make the necessary representation through the English legation in Sofia. To Gueshov,
Leishman claimed that Dickinson had written the April 5 letter to
Danev "against his [Leishman's] urgent advice and admonition."
Leishman told Gueshov that Dickinson sent the letter to test Bulgarian determination not to recognize him, and therefore should not be
accepted as an official representation of the American government.
Gueshov agreed and suggested to his foreign minister that the letter
be returned since it was "presented by a person who had no authority
to make such an 'official' petition to the Bulgarian government."[21]
While Leishman kept the State Department apprised of Bulgarian
objections, the department continued to refer to Dickinson as its
agent in Sofia until August, 1902.

The argument between Leishman and Dickinson over Dickinson's
official standing and Leishman's subsequent repudiation of Dickinson was only one in a series of disagreements that plagued their relationship. As described above, Leishman and Dickinson quarreled
over who had the right to negotiate, whose information was correct,
whose emissary was successful, and so on. Dickinson did, indeed,
blunder several times, especially in the dealings with the Bulgarian
government. But it seems that Leishman, by explaining events of the
kidnapping so as to protect himself from accusations of improper

conduct or negligence, exaggerated Dickinson's role and blamed him for things he had not done. Thus, Leishman said Dickinson and House had accepted impossible demands on the American government as conditions for Stone and Tsilka's release, and Dickinson had given the Porte the impression that the legation was trying to hinder Turkish investigations into the affair.[22]

Leishman was intent on proving to the State Department that he had managed to keep hidden United States government involvement in the negotiations for the release of Stone and Tsilka. He went so far as to claim that it was plain to the brigands that the Missionary Society was ransoming one of their members, "Mr. Gargiulo merely being there to facilitate their movement." This allowed Leishman to write that the "Government is absolutely free to take any action it may deem proper."[23]

Leishman's pretense of uninvolvement did not fool the Ottoman government. Immediately following Stone's and Tsilka's release, Turkish officials began to blame the United States legation for hindering attempts to track down and capture the band by insisting on reduced patrols and diminished troop activity. When Leishman complained that Turkish measures were not "as thorough as could be desired," Turkish officials retorted that appropriate measures were impossible because of earlier American requests which effectively prevented the Turks from gathering information which would lead to the capture of the band. By mid-August, 1902, Turkish officials actually disputed whether Stone was really captured on Ottoman territory in the first place. In a letter to Leishman, the foreign minister twisted the few known facts of the case in such a manner as to prove that Stone had been captured in Bulgaria and had remained there with her captors until the ransom was paid. Exaggerating the requests made by the legation to facilitate payment of the ransom, the foreign minister declared that compliance with these demands absolved the Porte of all liability for the kidnapping.[24]

The State Department steadfastly refused to consider the question of responsibility until Stone was released. There was no doubt, however, that the United States was committed to reimbursing the contributors to the ransom fund or that it had the right to demand an indemnity from whomever was judged the guilty party. Immediately after the women's release, the department addressed the question of responsibility, instructing Leishman on March 5 to gather reports from all parties having knowledge of facts about the kidnapping,

captivity, and ransoming of Stone and Tsilka. The department specifically wanted to know about previous kidnappings, whether Stone's
abduction was part of a general scheme, and what authorities, if any,
had been negligent in their duties, thus allowing the kidnapping to
occur.

Most people held Turkey legally responsible for the kidnapping:
the women, when captured, had been travelling with Turkish pass-
ports on Turkish territory, and the payment of the ransom and the
subsequent release of the women had all occurred on Turkish territory. And obvious precedents existed of the Ottoman government
ransoming foreigners who had been kidnapped on her territory.[25]
Yet opinion was divided on whether the United States had a strong
case against Turkey or whether Bulgaria was responsible, to some
degree, either through negligence in controlling the Macedonian
committees or through her "lack of cooperation" in the early stages
of the affair.

The missionaries, in particular, divided over the question of responsibility. The secretary of the American Board, Judson Smith,
got the impression from his dealings with the State Department that
an indemnity would be requested from Turkey. Peet supported
Smith, believing that the United States had a strong case against
Turkey and should immediately lodge its claim for repayment. Other
missionaries in the area were not quite as sure that Turkey should
be held responsible. Washburn advised the United States not to press
its claim against Turkey because it had hindered Ottoman efforts to
capture the band by demanding the withdrawal of troops from the
area in which Stone was kidnapped.[26] Others, such as Haskell and
Clarke in Samokov and Thomson (who had been stationed in Samokov for many years before his transfer to Edinburgh), believed that
Bulgaria deserved to be held to account for the affair because of its
support of Macedonian terrorism. Still others, while condemning the
methods of the Macedonian committee, sympathized with the Macedonian cause, and therefore did not think the United States should
press its claims against the Bulgarian government, or even charge the
government openly with culpability in the affair. One of the missionaries in Plovdiv thought it inadvisable to press a claim against either
Bulgaria or Turkey because Stone was to blame for her "imprudence
in holding her summer school in Macedonia and for travelling without a guard."[27]

House, the missionary most intimately involved, offered no advice
as to where to lay the blame. His only suggestion was that the United

States should deal directly with Bulgaria if the latter was judged guilty and not try to punish Bulgaria by letting the Turks take revenge on the Bulgarian population of Macedonia. House, much later, expressed the opinion that while Turkey was legally responsible, a claim should not be pressed because such a move would not punish the brigands who were the guilty party, but instead would play into their hands.[28]

Stone, as has been mentioned before, believed that the Ottoman government was responsible for paying the indemnity. For years she tried to prevail on Washington to press its claims against the Turks. She wrote letters to senators, to the secretary of state, and to the president. The American Board neither supported nor criticized her efforts because the board felt the money had been raised without its "official" participation; therefore whether the State Department collected an indemnity and repaid the contributors was none of the board's business.[29]

American officials were no more able to resolve the question of responsibility or decide how to punish Stone's captors than the missionaries. Leishman, in particular, expressed a number of contradictory positions and wavered between blaming the Turks and making excuses for them. Before Stone was freed, he stated, the Turks, on the whole, had "acted very generously and rendered assistance" when requested. He recommended not pressing a claim against Turkey because such an act would be a sign of friendliness which the Turks would greatly appreciate. Yet, a few weeks later, after Stone's release, Leishman accused the Ottoman military authorities of deliberately violating American agreements with the Porte, in which case the Porte indeed stood guilty of negligence and responsibility for the affair.[30]

Leishman later softened this position, saying that Turkey could not really be considered negligent or be blamed for an affair that occurred in Macedonia, an area over which they had little, if any, control. The scene of Stone's kidnapping was, according to Leishman, an area in which a "yearly revolution" was common. It was difficult, if not impossible, to pursue the brigands through that area. Moreover, the local population certainly would describe any movement of Ottoman troops as an "act of oppression" and use such movement as a pretext for an uprising. Although Leishman in his communications with the State Department recommended that no claim be pressed against Turkey, he continued to prod Ottoman officials to capture and punish the kidnappers with threats of an indemnity.[31] As far as the Bulgarian government was concerned, Leishman was sure it was in no way involved in the affair and considered rumors to that effect "cruel" and "unfair."[32] The only thing Leishman held against the Bulgarian government was its inability to arrest Boris Sarafov, but he attributed that to the fact that the government was young and weak and could not detain so influential a man just on suspicion.[33] Since Leishman was unable to prove that the members of the band were Bulgarian citizens or that they had been supported by the Sofia-based Macedonian committee, he concluded that it was impossible to hold the Bulgarian government liable for the indemnity.

Oddly enough, Dickinson made the same recommendation. According to Gueshov, Dickinson changed his attitude toward the Bulgarian government because Stone had been released in Turkey, a great distance from the Bulgarian border.[34] More likely, Dickinson, while continuing to suspect Bulgarian involvement, felt certain it would be impossible to obtain the conviction or imprisonment of any person in Bulgaria or to prove the complicity of the Bulgarian government. Such failures, Dickinson believed, would impair the prestige of the United States, and the attempt was not worth the effort.[35]

From all these contradictory suggestions, the State Department had to decide who was responsible. As early as February 26, 1902, a memorandum from the solicitor general of the State Department stated that the evidence pointed to "cooperative action by the Turks and weakness and culpability of the Bulgarians"; it also noted that presentation of a claim to Turkey would further the objectives of the Macedonian committee, and it tentatively recommended that a claim, if made, should be addressed to Bulgaria.[36] The secretary of state, John Hay, refused to act until all possible evidence had been collected, but even after receiving statements from all the participants, he could still come to no decision. On one hand, American officials in Washington maintained privately that Bulgaria was responsible, above all, and that a claim against Turkey would play into the hands of the Bulgarian government by pointing out the negligence of Ottoman officials in Macedonia. On the other hand, no solid basis existed on which to blame the Bulgarian government, and the American officials carefully kept their suspicions to themselves. On January 19, 1905, Secretary of State Hay decided that "it was not advisable to attempt to hold the Turkish government responsible" for the capture or to secure the repayment of the money from Turkey. Hay again declined to press any claim in April of that year. Under pressure from Stone, the State Department again reviewed the available evidence, and on March 24, 1908, concluded it could take no action against Turkey.

Stone then began to campaign to get Congress to appropriate money to repay contributors to the ransom fund. Secretary of State Elihu Root supported her in a letter, officially notifying President Roosevelt that the State Department could not fix responsibility. Root noted that the department had assured contributors that as a last resort, Congress would repay them, and this assurance had been "instrumental in enabling Miss Stone's friends to secure the sum of $66,000." Root concluded that the executive branch seemed "bound to make good its promise to recommend to Congress that money be appropriated," and he advised the president to do so immediately.[37]

Between 1908 and 1912, the Senate four times passed legislation authorizing repayment of the money raised to ransom Ellen Stone, but the bill never cleared the House of Representatives. Finally on May 21, 1912, Congress passed a bill "enabling the Secretary of State to return to such contributors as may file their claims within two years from the passage of this act, the money raised to pay the ransom for the release of Miss Ellen M. Stone, an American missionary to Turkey, who was abducted by brigands on September third, nineteen hundred and one."[38]

The kidnapping of Ellen Stone and Katerina Tsilka brought once again to world attention the inflammatory conditions in Macedonia. It exacerbated the underlying conflict between the Christian population and its Moslem rulers, but failed to strengthen IMRO as Sandansky and Chernopeev had envisioned. Ottoman repression of IMRO members and competition from the supreme committee prevented the organization from using the ransom money to attain control of the revolutionary movement in Macedonia. IMRO frittered away the money against its rival and failed to prepare for an uprising against the Turks. The Ilinden Uprising in August, 1903, called against the advice of Delchev, Petrov, Sandansky, Chernopeev, and many others, was crushed within a few months by the Ottoman authorities. Instead of liberation from the Turks, it brought severe reprisals against the Bulgarian population, disintegration of IMRO chapters in Macedonia, and debilitating factions to the Macedonian movement.

With Gotse Delchev's death in a Turkish ambush in early 1903, Yane Sandansky assumed leadership of the "left wing" of IMRO. He was assassinated in 1915. Khristo Chernopeev supported Sandansky in his battle against IMRO's other factions and against the supreme committee. He also took part in the Young Turk uprising against Abdul Hamid in 1912, fought with the Bulgarian army in the Balkan Wars, and was a representative to the Bulgarian National Assembly from 1914 until his death from natural causes in October 1915.

Ellen Stone's name was long retained as a staff member of the Protestant mission in Salonika, although she never returned there. With the passage through Congress of the legislation to repay contributors to her ransom fund, Stone devoted her time to lecturing on behalf of the Women's Christian Temperance Union. She died in Chelsea, Massachusetts on December, 1927.

The Tsilkas returned to Kortcha, Albania with their new baby, Elena, still suspected by the Ottoman authorities of complicity in the kidnapping. To avoid further persecution during the Ilinden Uprising, the Tsilkas escaped with the help of the Austrian consul in Bitola and made their way to the United States in the summer of 1903. There Katerina Tsilka earned a great deal of money on the summer Chatauqua circuit, lecturing on the "political and economic condition of Turkey, brigandage and her experiences with Miss Stone" and exhibiting baby Elena. American audiences received her with enthusiasm. She was, according to one set of program notes, "not so serious and matter of fact as Miss Stone; she has more sentiment and a keener sense of humor, and her lectures appeal more keenly to the average audience because she is younger, better looking and there is a tinge of romance in her career." When she brought the baby Elena out, the audiences went "wild."[39]

The Tsilkas returned to Albania after their successes in the United States; Grigor, once again, establishing a Protestant parish and school. Katerina bore another daughter and two sons, dying in 1952 in Tirana at the age of 86. The "lucky one," Elena, was by all accounts, as intelligent as she was beautiful. She attended the Protestant college in Constantinople, Robert College, marrying right after graduation the American consul in Tirana, George Minor. But she had tuberculosis; a tour through the major sanitoriums of Europe failed to cure it, and she died at the age of twenty-four in Tirana.

NOTES

Chapter I

1. The Constantinople Conference is discussed by Mihail D. Stoyanovic, *The Great Powers and the Balkans* (London: Cambridge Univ. Press, 1939), pp. 95-145; and Francis Seymour Stevenson, ed., *The Macedonian Question* (London: The Byron Society, 1902).

2. Michael Hurst, ed., *Key Treaties for the Great Powers, 1814-1914* (New York: St. Martin's Press, 1972), II, pp. 562-63.

3. The Organic Law of Crete, promulgated after the Cretan Uprising of 1866-67, designated Crete as a separate administrative region (vilayet), divided into five provinces and subdivided into nineteen districts. The governor-general, a Moslem, was to have two advisers, one Christian, one Moslem. Each provincial governor, if a Christian, had a Moslem assessor, and vice versa, and was assisted by a local administrative council. A general assembly, elected from each district, dealt with "measures of public utility." Official correspondence was conducted in both Greek and Turkish and religious questions were decided only by those involved. The Organic Law was meant to give a role in local administration to the Christian population, religious freedom, and recognition of national differences which existed between the Turks and the Greeks. William Miller, *The Ottoman Empire and Its Successors, 1801-1927* (London: Cambridge Univ. Press, 1927), pp. 314-15.

4. "Document No. 181," *Documents and Materials on the History of the Bulgarian People* (Sofia: Bulgarian Academy of Sciences, Institute of History, 1969), pp. 223-24. (The compilation will hereafter be cited as *Documents and Materials.*)

5. "Document No. 189," *Documents and Materials*, pp. 233-34. The dioceses included Debar, Ohxrid, Locktur, Lerin, Bitola, Voden, Melnik, Serres, Drama, Dorpa, Velles, Skopje, Palanka, Dzhumaia, Shtip, and others.

6. "Document No. 190," *Documents and Materials*, pp. 234-36.

7. Xristo Silyanov, *Ilindenskoto vüstanie*, Vol. I of *Osvoboditelni borbi na Makedoniya* (Sofia: Dürdezhavna Pechatnitsa, 1933), p. 40.

8. *Kresnensko-Razloshkoto vustanie, 1878. Dokumenti i drugi materiali* (Sofia: Bulgarian Academy of Sciences, 1970).

9. Liubimir Miletich, "Spomeni na Xristo Tatarchev," Vol. IX of *Materiali za Istoriyata na Makedonskoto Osvoboditelno Dvidzhenie* (Sofia: P. Glushkov, 1928), pp. 101-03. Miletich collected the memoirs of individuals involved in the Macedonian liberation movement in nine volumes which were published in Sofia in 1927 and 1928.

10. Miletich, "Spomeni na Damian Gruev," Vol. V of *Materiali*, p. 11.

11. Miletich, "Spomeni na Xristo Tatarchev," Vol. IX of *Materiali*, p. 103. The statutes of the 1867 Committee are published in Zakhari Stoyanov, *Zapiski po Bŭlgarskite Vŭstaniya* (1884: rpt. Sofia, Bulgarskite Pisateli, 1977), pp. 98-108.

12. Miletich, "Spomeni na Damian Gruev," Vol. V of *Materiali*, p. 111.

13. Khristo Shaldev, "Iz zapiskite na Ivan Xadzhinikolov," *Ilustratsia Ilinden*, No. 1 (1936), pp. 4-5.

14. Peter Poparcov, "Proizxod na revoliutsionnoto dvizhenie v Makedoniya i pŭrvite stŭpki na Soliunskiya 'Komitet' za pridobi vane politicheski prava na Makedoniya, dadeni i ot Berlinskiya dogovor," *Biuletin na Vremenoto Predstavitelstvo* [Sofia] No. 8, July 19, 1919, 2.

15. Miletich, "Spomeni na Xristo Tatarchev," Vol. IX of *Materiali*, p. 102.

16. These local committees in Shtip served as models for future groups. In the swearing-in ceremony, each member pledged that he would work with all his might for the liberation of Macedonia, would fulfill all tasks assigned to him, and would maintain strict secrecy. Each member accepted that if he broke his vow or revealed any secrets, he would be killed with a weapon which he had first kissed. After the ceremony, each member was given a code number and assigned to a group of ten. Siliyanov, *Ilindenskoto Vŭstanie*, p. 42.

17. Siliyanov, *Ilindenskoto Vŭstanie*, p. 42.

18. Miletich, "Spomeni na Yane Sandansky," Vol. V. of *Materiali*, p. 14.

19. Information about the Salonika Congress is mainly from the memoirs of Georcho Petrov. Miletich, Vol. VIII of *Materiali*, pp. 50-51.

20. The "Statutes" and "Rules and Regulations" are published in Konstantin Pandev, "Ustavi i pravilnitsi na VMORO predi Ilindenskoto-Preobradzhenskoto vŭstanie," *Izvestiya na Instituta za Istoriya*, 21 (1970), 249-57. (Hereafter cited as Pandev, "Ustavi i pravilnitsi.")

21 For the development of the legal Macedonian movement in Bulgaria see Siliyanov, *Ilindenskoto Vŭstanie*, pp. 48-49.

22. Iordan Ivanov, ed., *Sŭchineniya na Traiko Kitanchev* (Sofia: 1898), pp. 52-55.

23. *Glas Makedonski*, 22 (May 7, 1895); *Pravo* 25 (May 9, 1895).

24. The most important incident was the attack on Melnik, led by a second lieutenant, Boris Sarafov, later to become chairman of the supreme committee. Siliyanov, *Ilindenskoto Vüstanie*, pp. 56-58.

25. Silyanov, *Ilindenskoto Vüstanie*, pp. 59-60; Miletich, "Spomeni na Damian Gruev," Vol. V of *Materiali*, pp. 19-20.

26. Peyo K. Yavorov, "Gotse Delchev," Vol. III of *Süchineniya* (1909 rpt., Sofia: Bülgarskite Pisateli, 1965), pp. 167, 170-71.

27. Miletich, "Spomeni na Georcho Petrov," Vol. VIII of *Materiali*, pp. 44-45.

28. Miletich, "Spomeni na Georcho Petrov," Vol. VIII of *Materiali*, pp. 46-47.

29. Miletich, "Spomeni na Georcho Petrov," Vol. VIII of *Materiali*, p. 57.

30. Miletich, "Spomeni na Georcho Petrov," Vol. VIII of *Materiali*, p. 45.

31. Pandev, "Ustavi i pravilnitsi," pp. 245-77.

32. Miletich, "Spomeni na Ivan Anastasov Gercheto," Vol. VII of *Materiali*, pp. 110-11.

33. Miletich, Vol. VIII of *Materiali*, p. 61.

34. Lyubimir Miletich and Ivan Kharizanov are two examples. See the Introduction to Vol. VII of *Materiali*, p. 7; "Aferata Mis Ston," *Den*, I, No. 26 (Sept. 11, 1945).

35. Yavorov, "Gotse Delchev," p. 80.

36. Dino Küosev, ed., *Gotse Delchev, Pisma i Drugi Materiali* (Sofia: Bülgariskata Akademiya na Naukite, 1967), p. 65. A number of letters on following pages describe searches for the lost money.

37. Siliyanov, *Ilindenskoto Vüstanie*, pp. 89-90.

38. Yavorov, "Gotse Delchev," p. 183.

39. Miletich, "Spomeni na Boris Sarafov," Vol. V of *Materiali*, p. 47.

40. See Mandzhukov's description of the organization and equipping of the band that travelled with Gotse Delchev in 1899, in Simeon Simeonov, "Spomeni na P.G. Mandzhukov za uchastieto mu v cheta na Gotse Delchev prez 1899," *Izvestiya na Dürdzhavnite arxhivi, 23* (1972), p. 178. See also, letter of Gotse Delchev to prospective members of his band in Küosov, *Pisma*, pp. 171, 178.

41. Miletich, "Spomeni na Boris Sarafov," Vol. V of *Materiali*, pp. 38-40.

42. Küosov, *Pisma*, pp. 139, 141.

43. Yavorov, "Gotse Delchev," pp. 181-82.

44. Simeonov, "Spomeni na P. G. Mandzhukov," pp. 176, 181-91.

45. Yavorov, "Gotse Delchev," pp. 190-92.

46. Pandev, "Ustavi i pravilnitsi," pp. 265-71.

47. Siliyanov, *Ilindenskoto vŭstanie*, p. 104.

48, Miletich, Vol. V. of *Materiali*, p. 45.

49. Konstantin Pandev, "L'Organisation intèrieure et le Comité Suprème, 1899-1901," *Études Historiques*, Vol. VI (Sofia: Academie Bulgare des Sciences, Institut d'Histoire, 1973), pp. 230-31.

50. "Document No. 218," *Documents and Materials*, p. 272.

51. Ibid.

52. Miletich, "Predgovor," Vol. VII of *Materiali*, p. 6.

53. Bulgarian Academy of Sciences, Archives of the Institute of History, Collection IV, opus 192, archive unit 80, pp. 466-72.

54. Küosov, *Pisma*, pp. 305-315.

55. Kharizanov, "Aferata Mis Ston," *Den*, I, No. 26 (November 11, 1945), p. 3.

56. Kharizanov, "Aferata Mis Ston," *Den*, I, No. 27 (November 12, 1945), p. 4. Sandansky told Kharizanov the place he had picked for the capture of Ferdinand was ideal. Close to the village of Pastra, the road curved sharply and passed through a ravine whose edge was close enough to the Turkish border to make escape easy.

Chapter II

1. Yavorov, "Gotse Delchev," p. 70.

2. The suggestion has been attributed not only to Dimitur Lazarov but also to Dobri Daskalov, a former student at the Protestant school in Samokov and a member of Sandansky's band, to Dr. Khristo Dalkelechev, the IMRO committee chairman in Gevgeli, and even to Ellen Stone and Katerina Tsilka. See Kharizanov, "Aferata Mis Ston," *Den*, I, No. 26 (November 11, 1945); Peyu Chernopeev, *Dzhivot i Deinost na Khristo Chernopeev* (Sofia: Central Party Archive No. 2711). The latter is hereafter cited as P. Chernopeev, *Dzhivot i Deinost*.)

3. Ellen Stone, "Six Months Among Brigands," *McClure's Magazine*, XIX (May, 1902), p. 1.

4. Albert Sonnichsen, *Confessions of a Macedonian Bandit* (New York: Duffield, 1909), p. 259.

5. Paragraph II, No. 10 of the "Rules and Regulations for Bands" stated: "Political robberies and kidnappings could be executed only with authorization of the local regional committee in which the act was to take place and with permission of the Central Committee." Pandev, "Ustavi I Pravilnitsi," p. 266.

6. Lazar Tomov, *Spomeni za Revoliutsionnata Deinoct v Serskiya Okrŭg* (Sofia: Izdatelstvoto na Nationalnia Sevet na Otechestveniya Front, 1952), p. 18.

7. P. Chernopeev, *Dzhivot i Deinost*, p. 39.

8. Miletich, "Spomeni na Yane Sandansky," Vol. VII of *Materiali*, p. 86.

9. Unless otherwise noted, the account of Stone and Tsilka's captivity is from Ellen Stone, "Six Months Among Brigands," *McClure's Magazine*, XIX (May, June, July, September, and October, 1902), pp. 2-14, 99-109, 222-232, 464-471, 562-570; Elena Katerina Tsilka, "Born Among Brigands," *McClure's Magazine*, XIX (August, 1902), 291-300; P. Chernopeev, *Dzhivot i Deinost*; Ivan Kharizanov, "Aferata Mis Ston," *Den*, I, Nos. 26-37 (September 11-23, 1945).

10. Chernopeev insisted that the Turk was killed only because he was identified as the steward to a landlord who mercilessly squeezed the peasants and had himself raped two peasant girls. Sonnichsen, *Confessions,* p. 260.

11. According to Chernopeev, the band was so famished by the time they captured Stone that they did not have the presence of mind to refrain from eating pork. Sonnichsen, *Confessions*, p. 260.

12. Sonnichsen, *Confessions*, p. 260.

13. Miletich, "Spomeni na Sava Mikhailov," Vol. VII of *Materiali*, p. 87.

14. Telegram No. 387, Sestriicki to the Minister of Internal Affairs, 12/25 September, 1901, Bulgaria, Ministry of Foreign Affairs, Tsentralen Dürzhaven Istoricheski Arkhivi (Central Government Historical Archives), fund 176, opus 1, archive unit 1647, pp. 24-28 (The archives of the Bulgarian Foreign Ministry are hereafter cited as TDIA with the appropriate fund, opus, archive unit, and page number.)

Chapter III

1. Telegram No. 555, Lazzaro to Dickinson, September 5, 1901, enclosed in Report No. 73, Leishman to Hay, September 13, 1901, Diplomatic Dispatches, Turkey, General Records of the Department of State, Record Group 59, National Archives Microfilm Publications, M46, Role 68 May 7, 1901 to January 31, 1902 (Hereafter cited as M46, Role 68). A copy of Lazzaro's telegram to Dickinson can also be found in TDIA, fund 176, opus 1, archive unit 1647, pp. 16-18.

2. TDIA, fund 176, opus 1, archive unit 1647, pp. 1, 3, 6a.

3. Letter, Robert Thompson to James McGregor, September 13, 1901, enclosed in Report No. 79, Leishman to Hay, September 24, 1901, M46, Role 68.

4. For the Turkish view see Note Verbale, Commisariat Impériale Ottoman en Bulgare to Ministère des Affaires Étrangères, September 16, 1901, TSIA, fund 176, opus 1, archive unit 1647, p. 7; for the American view, Report No. 79, Leishman to Hay, September 24, 1902, M46, Role 68.

5. Telegram No. 619, Anton Shopov to Ivan St. Gueshov, September 1/14, 1901, TDIA, fund 176, opus 1, archive unit 1645, p. 5; Letter, Robert Thompson to the Chief of the Samokov Region, September 18, 1901, TDIA, fund 176, opus 1, archive unit 1647, p. 107.

6. Report No. 89, Eddy to Hay, October 2, 1901, M46, Role 68.

7. John H. House, "Facts with Reference to the Kidnapping, Captivity and Ransoming of Miss Ellen M. Stone: Official Report," March 20, 1902, American Farm School Archives, Salonika, Greece.

8. Report No. 556, September 5, 1901, enclosed in Report No. 73, Leishman to Hay, September 13, 1901, M46, Role 68.

9. Report No. 75 and Report No. 79, M46, Role 68.

10. Note Verbale No. 349, Commisariat Impériale Ottoman to Ministère des Affaires Étrangères, September 18, 1901, TDIA, fund 176, opus 1, archive unit 1647, p. 14.

11. Report No. 79, September 24, 1901, M46, Role 68.

12. Telegram No. 628, Shopov to Danev, September 5/18, 1901, TDIA, fund 176, opus 1, archive unit 1645, p. 9.

13. Bulgarian Series No. 2, Dickinson to Hay, August 1, 1901, Consular Dispatches, Constantinople, General Records of the Department of State, Record Group 59, National Archives Microfilm Publications, T682 1901 to 1904 (Hereafter cited as T682).

14. Bulgarian Series No. 3, Dickinson to Hay, August 31, 1901, T682.

15. Dickinson is referred to as diplomatic agent in Sofia as late as March, 1902.

16. Letters and telegrams, McGregor to Leishman, September 16, 19, and 20, 1901, enclosed in Report No. 79, Leishman to Hay, September 24, 1901, M46, Role 68.

17. It was indeed difficult for a foreign observer to understand the politics of the Macedonian movement. Representatives of foreign governments in Bulgaria and Turkey and the Turkish authorities did not differentiate between the Supreme Committee and IMRO. Instead, these representatives recognized the Bulgarian character of the population and the organization in Turkey and understood the final aim to be unification of the area with Bulgaria. The cooperation and unity of action during the chairmanship of Boris Sarafov reinforced

this impression. Sarafov gave the impression that the center of the movement was in Sofia and he stood at the head of the revolutionary organization.. If and when foreign representatives did differentiate between the revolutionary organizations, they generally saw only the contradictions between the two factions of the Supreme Committee in Sofia.

18. Telegram, Danev to Gueshov, September 5/18, 1901, TDIA, fund 176, opus 1, archive unit 1645, p. 6.

19. Vernazza added that no one ever attempted to blame the United States for the actions of her citizens abroad or to force her to arrest all anarchists living in the country. (He is probably referring to the assassination of King Umberto of Italy on July 29, 1900, by an American anarchist, Gaetano Bresci.) Notice B, Vernazzo to Sarafov, October 5/18, 1901, TDIA, fund 176, opus 1, archive unit 1647, pp. 101-102.

20. Telegram, Sarafov to Gueshov, September 19/October 5, 1901, TDIA, fund 176, opus 1, archive unit 1647, p. 38; Telegram, Sarafov to Stanchev, September 26/October 9, 1901, TDIA, fund 176, opus 1, archive unit 1647, p. 59.

21. Telegram, to Hay, September 23, 1901, M46, Role 68.

22. The State Department deemed it irrelevant that the Porte would, as in the past, repay the ransom. They also ignored the suggestions of missionaries in Constantinople that the band would settle for 2,000 to 3,000 lira. Report No. 89, Eddy to Hay, September 27, 1901, M46, Role 68.

23. Telegram, Adee to Smith, October 3, 1901; Telegrams, Adee to Eddy, October 4, 5, and 7, 1901. Diplomatic Instructions of the Department of State, Turkey. General Records of the Department of State, Record Group 59, National Archives Microfilm Publications, M77, Role 168, December 23, 1896 to June 5, 1902 (Hereafter cited as M77, Role 168). See also U.S. Congress, House, Committee on Claims, "Repayment of Ransom of Ellen Stone," H. Rept. 807, 62nd Cong., 2nd sess., (31 May, 1912), p. 2. A number of missionaries felt the matter could have been settled in a more satisfactory manner if the State Department had not authorized raising the ransom. See, for example, Missionary Herald, XCVII (November, 1901), 445.

24. Telegram, October 8, 1901, M77, Role 168.

25. Telegram, to Eddy, October 11, 1901, M77, Role 168.

26. Telegram, Adee to Dickinson, September 29, 1901, enclosed in Bulgarian Series No. 5, Dickinson to Adee, October 12, 1901, T682.

27. Telegram, Eddy to Hay, October 5, 1901, M46, Role 68; Telegrams, Hay to Dickinson, October 5 and 6, 1901, M77, Role 168; Bulgarian Series No. 5, Dickinson to Hay, October 12, 1901, T682.

28. Diplomatic Note No. 3, October 7, 1901, TDIA, fund 176, opus 1, archive unit 1647, pp. 48-50.

29. Diplomatic Note No. 4, TDIA, fund 176, opus 1, archive unit 1647, pp. 55-56. The note can also be found in Bulgarian Series No. 5, Dickinson to Hay, October 12, 1901, T682.

30. In Constantinople, Zinoviev told Eddy that he would "bring to bear full Russian influence to expostulate with the Bulgarian government to help Stone." In Sofia, Etter informed the Bulgarian government that he was instructed to give all help possible to Dickinson in his efforts to free Stone. Telegram, Eddy to Hay, October 5, 1901, M46, Role 68; Telegrams, Hay to Tower, October 3 and 5, 1901; Report No. 479, Tower to Hay, October 4, 1901; Report No. 480, Tower to Hay, October 7, 1901, Diplomatic Dispatches, Russia, General Records of the Department of State, Record Group 59, National Archives Microfilm Publications, M35, Role 58 March 1, 1901 to October 31, 1902 (Hereafter cited as M35, Role 58).

31. Telegrams, D. Stanchev to Danev, September 23 /October 6, 1901 and September 25/October 8, 1901, TDIA, fund 176, opus 1, archive unit 1647, pp. 40, 44.

32. Telegram, Eddy to Hay, October 8, 1901, M46, Role 68; Note Verbale No. 354, Danev to Impériale Commisariat Ottoman, October 4/17, 1901, TDIA, fund 176, opus 1, archive unit 1647, pp. 95-96; Telegram, Danev to D. Stanchev, September 26/October 9, 1901, TDIA, fund 176, opus 1, archive unit 1647, p. 59; Telegram, Danev to Gueshov, September 19/October 2, 1901, TDIA, fund 176, opus 1, archive unit 1647, p. 38.

33. Diplomatic Note No. 348, October 11, 1901, TDIA, fund 176, opus 1, archive unit 1647, pp. 77-79. The Bulgarian government was willing to pay an indemnity to Stone's family if anything should happen to her, rather than tolerate "the operations of outlaws." Notice, Vernazza to Sarafov, September 26/October 8, 1901, TDIA, fund 176, opus 1, archive unit 1647, pp. 157-78.

34. Telegram to Hay, October 14, 1901, T682.

35. Diplomatic Note No. 5, TDIA, fund 176, opus 1, archive unit 1647, p. 84.

36. Notice, Vernazza to Danev, October 5/18, 1901, TDIA, fund 176, opus 1, archive unit 1647, p. 100.

37. Telegram, Dickinson to Hay, October 14, 1901, T682.

38. Bulgarian Series No. 10, Dickinson to Hay, October 25, 1901, T682.

39. Bulgarian Series, No. 6, Dickinson to Hay, October 19, 1901, T682.

40. Bulgarian Series, No. 6, Dickinson to Hay, October 19, 1901, T682. Telegrams, Dickinson to Hay, October 8, 9, 10, 11, 12, and 13, 1901, T682.

41. Notice, Vernazza to Danev, September 25/October 8, 1901, TDIA, fund 176, opus 1, archive unit 1647, pp. 41-42.

42. There is no record of such a statement by a Bulgarian official.

43. Eddy falsely believed that Dickinson had ordered Lazzaro in Salonika to demand Turkish troop movements in conjunction with Bulgarian actions. This directly contradicted Eddy's request to the Turkish foreign minister for withdrawal of all troops in the area and made Eddy look very foolish. Dickinson, however, had never urged such an action and relative harmony was reestablished between Eddy and Dickinson. Telegrams, Eddy to Hay, October 9, 11, and 16, 1901, M46, Role 68.

44. Telegram, Tower to Hay, October 14, 1901, M35, Role 58.

45. Gueshov wired Danev on October 8 that Haskell had been charged by the American legation to offer 4,000 to 5,000 *lira* when he made contact, but there is no mention of this arrangement in American reports. TDIA, fund 176, opus 1, archive unit 1647, pp. 15-16.

46. Bulgarian Series No. 10, Dickinson to Hay, October 25, 1901, T682.

47. Telegram, Tower to Hay, October 27, 1901, M35, Role 58.

48. Asenov was away from the band at that time, returning October 29 with a letter for Stone. P. Chernopeev says Asenov and Chernopeev met with Haskell in Samokov before going to Sofia. P. Chernopeev, *Dzhivot i Deinost*, p. 102.

49. Telegram, Eddy to Hay, October 30, 1901, M46, Role 68.

50. The Bulgarian government learned of the negotiations even before Dickinson left for Samokov. Telegram, Gueshov to Danev, October 5/28, 1901, TDIA, fund 176, opus 1, archive unit 1645, p. 29.

51. Lazar Tomov, *Spomeni za Revoliütsionnata Deinost*, p. 22.

52. Stone, "Six Months Among Brigands," June 1902, p. 105.

53. Telegram, Dickinson to Hay, November 8, 1901, T682.

54. Kharizanov, "Aferata Mis Ston," *Den*, I, 32 (November 17, 1945), 3.

55. P. Chernopeev, *Dzhivot i Deinost*, p. 109.

56. Lazar Tomov, *Spomeni na Revoliütsionnata Deinost*, p. 23.

57. Telegram, Dickinson to Hay, November 8, 1901, T682.

58. Dickinson constantly refers to his "agent in Sofia" in later telegrams to the State Department, and Stone mentions Dickinson's agent in her memoirs.

59. Bulgarian Series No. 18, Dickinson to Hay, November 27, 1901, T682.

60. Telegrams, November 9 and 10, 1901, M46, Role 68.

61. Telegram, Eddy to Hay, November 26, 1901, M46, Role 68.

62. Telegram, Eddy to Hay, November 26, 1901, M46, Role 68; Notice, Vernazza to Sarafov, November 6/19, 1901, TDIA, fund 176, opus 1, archive unit 1647, pp. 149-50.

63. Bulgarian Series No. 9, Dickinson to Hay, October 22, 1901, T682.

64. Bulgarian Series No. 17, Dickinson to Hay, November 26, 1901, T682.

65. Bulgarian Series No. 11, Dickinson to Hay, November 17, 1901, T682.

66. Notice, Vernazza to Sarafov, November 6/19, 1901, TDIA, fund 176, opus 1, archive unit 1647, pp. 149-50.

67. Diplomatic Note No. 8, November 12, 1901, TDIA, fund 176, opus 1, archive unit 1647, pp. 137-40; Bulgarian Series No. 13, Dickinson to Hay, November 20, 1901, T682.

68. Diplomatic Note No. 7, October 23, 1901, T682.

69. Bulgarian Series No. 16, Dickinson to Hay, November 22, 1901, T682.

70. Telegram, Hay to Dickinson, November 9, 1901, T682.

71. Bulgarian Series No. 9, Dickinson to Hay, October 22, 1901; Telegrams, Dickinson to Hay, October 26 and 27, 1901, T682.

72. In fact, there seemed to be no further Russian involvement in the Stone affair until after it was over. No telegrams or messages relating to Stone appear in the correspondence between the American minister in St. Petersburg and the State Department from November 7, 1901 until March 19, 1902.

73. Notice, Vernazza to Sarafov, October 25/November 8, 1901, TDIA, fund 176, opus 1, archive unit 1647, pp. 133-133a.

74. Notice, Vernazza to Sarafov, October 27/November 10, 1901, TDIA, fund 176, opus 1, archive unit 1647, p. 135.

75. Diplomatic Note, November 14/27, 1901, TDIA, fund 176, opus 1, archive unit 1647, pp. 165-66.

76. Dispatch No. 386, November 17/30, 1901, TDIA, fund 176, opus 1, archive unit 1647, pp. 175-80.

Chapter IV

1. This chapter relies on the sources listed in note 9, Chapter II.

2. McKinley was shot by an anarchist on September 6, 1901. He died eight days later.

3. Stone's letter to her mother is published in Bulgarian in *Zornitsa*, 22, No. 10 (March 7, 1902), pp. 2-3.

4. The exact time of Doncho's attack is difficult to fix. P. Chernopeev claims it was in early November, but Stone says the attack took place after Thanksgiving. Neither Sandansky nor Kharizanov mentions a date. We know that Asenov and Chernopeev took part in repulsing the attack, not only from Sandansky's memoirs but also from Kharizanov and P. Chernopeev. As Chernopeev and Asenov were both in Sofia negotiating with Dickinson during early November, the raid could not have taken place with their participation. In addition, Stone says that Asenov did not return to the band until Thanksgiving Day, and upon his return the two women were taken to the two huts near Sushitsa. Kharizanov says the band intended to winter there, which seems reasonable because it would not be worth the trouble of building huts if they did not plan on spending a long period in them; there were many woodcutters' and shepherds' huts in that part of Macedonia. Sandansky admits that he and the women spent four days at Sushitsa, and that near there Doncho surrounded them. Thus, the attack must have been at the end of November near Troskovo.

How many men Doncho had—Kharizanov says 150, while Sandansky counted seventy-eight—and why he didn't press his advantage are questions impossible to answer.

Sandansky makes no reference in his memoirs to crossing into Bulgaria a second time. He states that after Doncho's attack, he took the women to Pokrovnik, while Chernopeev and Asenov went to Sofia. From Pokrovnik, Sandansky says he went to Serbinovo, arriving there on December 21 and from there headed to Vlakhi. From Stone's memoirs, however, it is clear that she and Tsilka were forced "to take long journeys night after night" right before the baby was born. The baby was born near Serbinovo, according to Kharizanov and P. Chernopeev, on January 4. If, as Sandansky claims, he and the group were in Serbinovo on December 21, they would have had little, if any, travelling to do before the birth of the baby. I have, therefore, followed the itinerary that P. Chernopeev describes, except for estimating the band's stay in Bulgaria as only about three weeks, not forty days as he claimed.

While everyone agrees that Asenov went back to Sofia, it is not clear what Chernopeev did. P. Chernopeev claims his father chased supreme committee bands during late December, but no one confirms this. Chernopeev and Asenov do not seem to have been with the band when the baby was born. See Miletich, "Spomeni na Yane Sandansky," Vol. VII of *Materiali*, pp. 20-21; P. Chernopeev, *Dzhivot i Deinost*, p. 57; Kharizanov, "Aferata Mis Ston," *Den*, I, Nos. 30 and 32; Stone, "Six Months Among Brigands," (June 1902), pp. 108-09.

5. Stone dates the letter "December 17-24, 1901," in a copy published in her memoirs. It is not clear why she used this dating. If she were using the old calendar, the date would be December 17/30, because there was a difference of thirteen days.

6. The baby was born around 10:00 P.M. on January 4, 1902.

Chapter V

1. See telegram, Eddy to Hay, November 27, 1901, M46, Role 68; Report No. 106, M. De Bensen to Lansdowne, December 3, 1901, Great Britain, *Correspondence Respecting the Affairs of South Eastern Europe: Turkey* (London, HMSO, 1903), I, p. 101; and Dispatch, December 30, 1901, Biliotti to Lansdowne, Archives of the Institute of History, Bulgarian Academy of Sciences, Collection, IV, opus 192, archive unit 52, p. 310.

2. Handwritten note dated December 10, 1901, attached to Bulgarian Series No. 15, Dickinson to Hay, November 20, 1901, T682. Leishman told Gueshov during January that he thought Dickinson had "made mistakes in Sofia which he shouldn't have." Telegram, Gueshov to Danev, January 9/22, 1902, TDIA, fund 176, opus 1, archive unit 1645, pp. 152-53.

3. Report No. 116 and No. 117, Eddy to Hay, December 13 and 15, 1901; and telegram, Eddy to Hay, December 21, 1901, M46, Role 68.

4. Memoradum of Washburn, enclosed in Report No. 117, Eddy to Hay, December 15, 1901; and telegram, Eddy to Hay, December 16, 1901, M46, Role 68.

5. Report No. 116, Eddy to Hay, December 13, 1901, M46, Role 68.

6. Telegram, Hay to Leishman, January 7, 1902, M46, Role 68.

7. Telegram, Gueshov to Danev, December 5/18, 1901, TDIA, fund 176, opus 1, archive unit 1647, pp. 185-86.

8. Telegram, Leishman to Gargiulo, January 12, 1902, enclosure No. 3 in Rpt. No. 146, Leishman to Hay, March 1, 1902, Diplomatic Dispatches, Turkey. General Records of the Department of State, Record Group 59, National Archives Microfilm Publications, M46, Role 69, February 3 to June 26, 1902 (Hereafter cited as M46, Role 69).

9. Dispatch No. 818, Shopov to Danev, December 9/22, 1901, TDIA, fund 176, opus 1, archive unit 1647, pp. 188-89.

10. Telegram, December 20, 1901, M46, Role 68.

11. Telegram, Hay to Dickinson, December 25, 1901, T682.

12. Telegram, Leishman to Hay, December 30, 1901, M46, Role 68.

13. Letter No. 131, Leishman to Dickinson, January 1, 1902, T682; Letter, Dickinson to Leishman, January 2, 1902, T682.

14. Letter, Dickinson to Leishman, January 2, 1902, T682.

15. Letter No. 139, Leishman to Dickinson, January 7, 1902, T682.

16. Statement of Gargiulo, April 6, 1902, enclosure No. 4 in Report No. 163, Leishman to Hay, April 12, 1902, M46, Role 69.

17. December 29, 1901, M46, Role 68.

18. Letter No. 521, Dickinson to Leishman, April 4, 1902, T682.

19. Telegram, Leishman to Hay, January 1, 1902, M46, Role 68.

20. Letter, Dickinson to Leishman, January 6, 1902, enclosure No. 1 in Report No. 123, Leishman to Hay, January 6, 1902, M46, Role 68.

21. Letter of January 1, 1902, T682.

22. Letter No. 139, Leishman to Dickinson, January 7, 1902, T682.

23. Statement of House, March 21, 1902, statement of Gargiulo, April 6, 1902, and statement of Peet, March 27, 1902, enclosed in Report No. 163, Leishman to Hay, April 12, 1902, M46, Role 69.

24. Todorov's letter to House reads: "Mr. J. H. House: As the authorized agent of Mr. Charles Dickinson to treat with the brigands for the ransoming and freeing of Miss Stone and Mrs. Tsilka, with this present I certify to the following:

1. The agent on the part of the brigands, with an authorization signed by Miss Stone and Mrs. Tsilka and I, the agent of Mr. Dickinson, have agreed that the captives shall be freed on the payment of a sum collected for this purpose, namely 14,500 *lira*.

2. As to exact place and manner of delivering the sum and freeing the captives you will agree with the person who will bring this letter from me. He has this right.

3. In order that you may be assured that the captives are alive and well, this, my letter, shall be put before Miss Stone and Mrs. Tsilka, that they may write with their own hands on the other side of this paper; after which it may be given to you.

4. A copy of this letter I am sending you by post.

5. The money may be paid in Napoleons."

On the back of the letter Todorov wrote: "Miss E. Stone: Write a few lines concerning things, incidents, or names which you and Mr. House know." Stone replied with comments about people they both knew and ended by saying Tsilka's baby had been born on January 4.

To Tsilka, Todorov addressed the following questions: "Answer who your friend was in East Orange, New Jersey, and who was the directress of the hospital in which you were."

Stone mistakenly dates this letter January 18 in her memoirs, thus making it appear that Todorov wrote two letters to House (besides the one Haskell delivered on January 3). It leads P. Chernopeev to claim that House sent Asenov, Sandansky, and Mikhailov back to the band after their first meeting to get a second endorsement from Stone and Tsilka dated January 18. From careful reading of her memoirs, it is obvious that this letter was read and endorsed on January 12, at the same time that she wrote an appeal to House to trust her captors. Both letters were handed to House in Bansko on January 16. Stone, "Six Months Among Brigands," (September, 1902), pp. 466-67.

25. Mikhailov joined the band in early January, 1902 because someone had revealed his membership in IMRO to the Ottoman authorities and he had to hide to escape arrest. Miletich, "Spomeni na Sava Mikhailov," Vol. VII of *Materiali*, p. 90. Sandansky says Chernopeev went off to fight the supreme committee bands while he went to Bansko. But according to Kharizanov, Chernopeev did not leave the band until after the ransom was paid. Miletich, "Spomeni na Yane Sandansky," Vol. VII of *Materiali*, p. 22; Kharizanov, "Aferata Mis Ston," *Den*, I, 34 (September 20, 1945), p. 3.

26. House spells it Egratchanoff in his "Official Report," American Farm School Archives, Salonika, Greece.

27. Report No. 124 and Report No. 127, M46, Role 68; Letter, Dickinson to Leishman, January 15, 1902, T682; Telegram, Gueshov to Danev, January 3/16, 1902, TDIA, fund 176, opus 1, archive unit 1762, p. 2.

28. Stone, "Six Months Among Brigands," (September, 1902), p. 468; Statement of House, March 21, 1902, enclosed in Report No. 163, Leishman to Hay, April 12, 1902, M46, Role 69.

29. Stone, "Six Months Among Brigands," (September, 1902), p. 468.

30. Telegram, Leishman to Hay, January 19, 1902, M46, Role 68.

31. Enclosure No. 1 in Report No. 129, Leishman to Hay, January 20, 1902, M46, Role 68.

32. Gargiulo to Leishman, January 20, 1902, in Report No. 134, Leishman to Hay, February 6, 1902, M46, Role 69.

33. The 15,000 *lira* would cover the ransom payment of 14,500 *lira* but would perhaps be inadequate for travelling expenses. Rather than excite curiosity by drawing more money on the department's account, Leishman advanced expense money from the legation treasury. Reports Nos. 129 and 130, Leishman to Hay, January 20, 1902, M46, Role 68.

34. Diplomatic Notes, Leishman to Tewfik, January 21 and 23, 1902; Diplomatic Note, Tewfik to Leishman, in Enclosure No. 2 in Report No. 134, Leishman to Hay, February 6, 1902, M46, Role 69. Unless otherwise noted, information on the shipment and payment of the ransom money and Ottoman interference with the progress of the negotiating committee is taken from telegrams between Gargiulo and Leishman from January 21 to February 6, 1902 and diplomatic notes between Leishman and Foreign Minister Tewfik during that same time period. Enclosures Nos. 1 and 2, respectively in Report No. 134, Leishman to Hay, February 6, 1902, M46, Role 69.

35. Letter, Smith-Lyte to Leishman, January 30, 1902, Enclosure No. 3 in Report No. 134, Leishman to Hay, February 6, 1902, M46, Role 69.

36. Diplomatic Note, Leishman to Tewfik, Enclosure No. 4 in Report No. 134, Leishman to Hay, February 6, 1902, M46, Role 69.

37. Enclosure No. 3 in Report No. 134, Leishman to Hay, February 6, 1902, M46, Role 69.

38. None of the accounts of the affair explain how Sandansky, Asenov, and Mikhailov managed to slip through the Turkish blockade. Presumably they were disguised as local peasants.

39. Sandansky says the ransom was paid on January 18, or January 31 in the new calendar, but he dictated his memoirs five or six years after the kidnapping and his memory was not accurate.

40. House, Peet, and Gargiulo were shadowed constantly, not only by Turkish soldiers but also by a number of English correspondents. The most persistent of these, William Maud, a reporter for the London magazine, *Daily Graphic*, along with an artist who also worked for the magazine, had joined Peet and Gargiulo in Serres. The latter two refused to let Maud and his colleague travel with them and secretly left the city for Gorna Dzhumaia. Maud asked for but was refused a guard to travel with him by the Serres authorities, and he travelled at his own risk after the negotiating committee. Telegram, Shopov to Danev, January 4/17, 1902, TDIA, fund 176, opus 1, archive unit 1762, p. 3.

41. J. M. Nankivell, *A Life for the Balkans: The Story of John Henry House of the American Farm School*, (New York: Fleming H. Revell, 1939), p. 139; Miletich, "Spomeni na Yane Sandansky," Vol. VII of *Materiali*, p. 23.

42. Gerasim N. Popov, "Shestdeset godini na plenyavaneto na Elena Mis Ston, 1901-1961," (Velingrad, Bulgaria, 25 August, 1961); Kharizanov, "Aferata Mis Ston," *Den*, I, No. 34 (19 November, 1945); Anton Strashmimiov, *Krüstio Asenov*, (Sofia: n.p., 1906), p. 234.

43. Quoted in P. Chernopeev, *Dzbivot i Deinost*, p. 153.

44. P. Chernopeev, *Dzivot i Deinost*, pp. 152-54.

45. Nankivell, *A Life for the Balkans*, p. 139.

46. Frederick Moore, *The Balkan Trail*, (London: Smith, Elder and Co., 1906), p. 39.

47. Nankivell, *A Life for the Balkans*, p. 139.

48. Stone, "Six Months Among Brigands," (September, 1902), p. 469.

49. Miletich, "Spomeni na Yane Sandansky," Vol. VII of *Materiali*, p. 23; P. Chernopeev, *Dzbivot i Deinost*, p. 166.

50. Yavorov, *Gotse Delchev*, p. 208; Kharizanov, "Aferata Mis Ston," *Den*, I, No. 36 (November 21, 1945), p. 3; P. Chernopeev, *Dzbivot i Deinost*, p. 167.

51. P. Chernopeev, *Dzbivot i Deinost*, p. 167.

52. Miletich, "Spomeni na Sava Mikhailov," Vol. VII of *Materiali*, p. 92; Kharizanov, "Aferata Mis Ston," *Den*, I, No. 35 (21 November, 1945), p. 3; Sonnichsen, *Confessions*, p. 265; P. Chernopeev, *Dzbivot i Deinost*, p. 167.

53. Whether there is any truth to Gargiulo's accusation is hard to determine. In a letter to Leishman of February 8, House implies he did translate for Peet and Gargiulo. He gave as an example trying to translate Gargiulo's explanation of the "difficulty of Tsilka's case as she was not an American citizen." Gargiulo promised to do "what was possible for her." Enclosure No. 3 in Report No. 146, Leishman to Hay, March 1, 1902, M46, Role 69.

54. Statement of House, March 21, 1902, in Report No. 163, Leishman to Hay, April 12, 1902, M46, Role 69.

55. Telegram, Leishman to Gargiulo, February 16, in Report No. 146, Leishman to Hay, March 1, 1902; Letter, Leishman to House, March 26, in Report No. 163, Leishman to Hay, April 12, 1902, M46, Role 69.

56. Telegram, Shopov to Danev, January 30/February 12, 1902, TDIA, fund 176, opus 1, archive unit 1762, p. 25; Letters, Biliotti to O'Connor, February 13 and 17, 1902, Archives of the Institute of History, Bulgarian Academy of Sciences, Collection IV, opus 192, archive unit 74, p. 454 and archive unit 80, pp. 466-72.

57. Telegram, Gueshov to Danev, January 22/February 4, 1902, TDIA, fund 176, opus 1, archive unit 1645, pp. 62-63.

58. Diplomatic Note, Leishman to Tewfik, February 5, 1902, Enclosure No. 2 in Report 134, Leishman to Hay, February 6, 1902, M46, Role 69.

59. It might seem unusual that Leishman agreed to notify the Turkish government of the payment of the ransom (a decision that changed the situation considerably) without asking permission or receiving instructions from the State Department. However, both Leishman and the State Department were bent on distancing themselves from the day-to-day workings of the affair in order to keep up the fiction that the United States government was not involved. Gargiulo told Leishman only the essential facts that Leishman needed to deal with the Turks, and Leishman, in turn, passed on only the little he knew to the State Department. Copies of Gargiulo's telegrams to Leishman and Leishman's notes to Minister Tewfik for the period February 6 to March 1, 1902, are contained in Enclosures Nos. 1 and 2 of Report No. 146, Leishman to Hay, March 1, 1902, M46, Role 69.

60. Telegrams, Shopov to Danev, February 3/16, 5/18 and 6/19, 1902, TDIA, fund 176, opus 1, archive unit 1645, p. 73; archive unit 1762, p. 28; and archive unit 1762, p. 29.

61. Diplomatic Note, Tewfik to Leishman, February 14, 1902, Enclosure No. 2, in Report No. 146, Leishman to Hay, March 1, 1902, M46, Role 69.

62. Telegrams, Leishman to Gargiulo, February 16, 19, and 20, 1902, Enclosure No. 1 in Report No. 146, Leishman to Hay, March 1, 1902, M46, Role 69.

63. Precisely why Chernopeev did not take the women to the district of Serres as had been agreed between Sandansky and the negotiating committee is not clear. Possibly, he was not told of the agreement; possibly, he considered the route too dangerous. Unfortunately, it is a question none of the participants ever discussed.

64. Stone, "Six Months Among Brigands," (September and October, 1902), pp. 470-71 and 562-66.

Chapter VI

1. Reports Nos. 145 and 163, Leishman to Hay, March 5 and April 2, 1902, M46, Role 69.

2. Statement of the Reverend James W. Baird, March 13, 1902, Enclosure No. 5 in Rpt. No. 163, Leishman to Hay, April 12, 1902, M46, Role 69.

3. Telegram No. 176, Shopov to Gueshov, March 26/April 8, 1902, TDIA, fund 176, opus 1, archive unit 1762, p. 52.

4. Stone, "Six Months Among Brigands," (October, 1902), pp. 565-70. The local police commissioner evidently misunderstood much of what Stone and Tsilka told him. His report was full of errors and the mayor discarded it.

5. There were a number of newspapers and magazines interested in publishing an account of Stone's experiences. Even before her release, *McClure's Magazine* had left an offer for her with Dickinson of $5,000 for an exclusive account. After her release, Stone agreed to accept $8,000 (part of it went to Tsilka for the article she wrote) and $35,000 for a series of fifty-four lectures throughout the United States. Stone was accused of filling her own pockets and of getting more money from her kidnapping than her kidnappers. She defended herself by saying the money was to be used to build an industrial school in some city in Macedonia. See documents in the American Farm School Archives, Salonika, Greece; Rpt. No. 146, Leishman to Hay, March 1, 1902, M46, Role 69; Dispatch No. 115, Shopov to Danev, February 22/March 7, 1902, TSIA, fund 176, opus 1, archive unit 1645, p. 88; *Zornitsa*, Nos. 18 and 44, May 2 and October 31, 1902.

6. Dispatch No. 182, Shopov to Danev, February 18/March 3, 1902, TDIA, fund 176, opus 1, archive unit 1645, pp. 86-87.

7. Dispatch No. 39, Shopov to Danev, January 17/30, 1902, TDIA, fund 176, opus 1, archive unit 1645, p. 18; Rpt. No. 145, Leishman to Hay, March 5, 1902, M46, Role 69.

8. Dispatch No. 129, Shopov to Danev, February 26/March 11, 1902, TDIA, fund 176, opus 1, archive unit 1645, p. 87; Letter, Biliotti to Lansdowne, February 26, 1902, Archives of the Institute of History, Bulgarian Academy of Sciences, Collection IV, opus 135, archive unit 21, pp. 86-90.

9. Letter, Baird to House, March 10, 1902, American Farm School Archives, Salonika, Greece; Letter, Haskell to the American Board of Foreign Missions, December 5, 1902, quoted in William Webster Hall, *Puritans in the Balkans*, (Sofia: Studia Historico-Philologica Serdicensia, Supplement, Vol. I, 1938), p. 164; Rpt. No. 155, Leishman to Hay, March 22, 1902, M46, Role 69.

10. Dispatch No. 101, Shopov to Danev, February 16/March 1, 1902, TDIA, fund 176, opus 1, archive unit 1762, pp. 41-43; Dispatch No. 261, Gueshov to Danev, February 12/25, 1902, TDIA, fund 176, opus 1, archive unit 1762, pp. 37-38.

11. "Six Months Among Brigands," (October, 1902), p. 570.

12. On March 29, 1902, Tsilka wrote Leishman asking if there was "any possibility of shortening our case with the government. . . .

They keep us here without doing anything." Leishman did not respond to this letter. Enclosure No. 1 in Rpt. 163, Leishman to Hay, April 12, 1902, M46, Role 69.

13. Kharizanov, "Aferata Mis Ston," *Den*, I, Nos. 35 and 36 (November 21 and 22, 1945), pp. 3, 4.

14. House, "The Capture of Miss Stone and the Missionary Work," American Farm School Archives, Salonika, Greece; Rpt. No. 122, Leishman to Hay, January 1, 1902, M46, Role 69; Diplomatic Note No. 143, Leishman to Tewfik, July 18, 1902, Enclosure No. 3 in Rpt. No. 233, Leishman to Hay, July 18, 1902, M46, Role 69.

15. Rpt. No. 155, Leishman to Hay, March 22, 1902, M46, Role 69.

16. Letter No. 154, Leishman to Dickinson, (undated), in Rpt. No. 138, Leishman to Hay, February 26, 1902, M46, Role 69.

17. Letter No. 510, Dickinson to Leishman, April 8, 1902, T682.

18. Notice of Vernazza, February 7/20, 1902, TDIA, fund 176, opus 1, archive unit 1762, p. 30. These instructions were repeated on February 11/24, 1902. TDIA, fund 176, opus 1, archive unit 1762, p. 34.

19. On February 18, the Bulgarian minister in St. Petersburg, Stanchev, sent the American minister, Tower, a note asking for the appointment of a new American diplomatic agent to Sofia. The Bulgarian foreign minister, Danev, reiterated this position to Tower in person while on a visit to St. Petersburg in early April. Danev asked Tower to communicate the "sincere wishes of the Bulgarian government to establish permanent diplomatic relations" with the United States. The Bulgarian government had no objection to an agent accredited to another Balkan state or Greece, but could not accept anyone accredited to Turkey. Rpts. Nos. 549 and 560, Tower to Hay, March 19 and April 8, 1902, Diplomatic Dispatches, Russia, General Records of the Department of State, Record Group 59, National Archives Microfilm Publications, M35, Role 59, November 1, 1901 to December 20, 1902.

20. Gueshov to Leishman, March 15/28, 1902, in Rpt. No. 158, Leishman to Hay, March 29, 1902, M46, Role 69.

21. Dispatch No. 585, Gueshov to Acting Foreign Minister Liudkanov, March 29/April 11, 1902, TDIA, fund 176, opus 1, archive unit 1762, pp. 48-49.

22. On March 22, the Ministry of Foreign Affairs requested Leishman to direct Stone to appear before Ottoman authorities in Salonika. A misunderstanding arose because Stone thought Gargiulo had told her not to appear, and Dickinson relayed this information to the *Vali* of Salonika, making it appear that the legation was not cooperating

in the Ottoman investigation. This misunderstanding contributed further to Leishman's dislike of Dickinson. Telegram, Leishman to Hay, March 22, 1902; Letter, Leishman to Stone, March 25, 1902 in Rpt. No. 157, Leishman to Hay, March 28, 1902, M46, Role 69; Letters Nos. 173 and 175, Leishman to Dickinson, March 22 and 24, 1902; Letter No. 505, Dickinson to Leishman, March 24, 1902, T682.

23. Rpt. No. 155, Leishman to Hay, March 22, 1902, M46, Role 69.

24. Dispatch No. 261, Gueshov to Danev, February 12/25, 1902, TDIA, fund 176, opus 1, archive unit 1762, pp. 37-38; Rpt. No. 233, Leishman to Hay, July 19, 1902, M46, Role 69; Letters, Tewfik to Leishman, July 13 and August 28, 1902, in Rpt. No. 269, Leishman to Hay, September 6, 1902, Diplomatic Dispatches, Turkey, General Archives of the Department of State, Record Group 59, National Archives Microfilm Publications, M46, Role 70, July 1 to December 29, 1902 (Hereafter cited ad M46, Role 70).

25. The first such case occurred in 1880 in the district of Salonika when an English army colonel named Synge was kidnapped. The English government paid his ransom of 10,000 *lira* and then deducted that sum from money due Turkey by England. There were another fifteen kidnappings of French, Italian, and British citizens on Ottoman territory between Colonel Synge's and Ellen Stone's kidnappings. In six of the cases, the Ottoman government paid the ransom to the kidnappers through intermediaries, and in one case, reimbursed the government that had paid the ransom. In two cases, the Porte declined all responsibility for the affair; once because the kidnapping was judged a case of "personal vengeance" and the other for no specific reason. The majority of the cases were pure brigandage, in no way political. Enclosure No. 9 in Rpt. No. 163, Leishman to Hay, April 12, 1902, M46, Role 69.

26. Quoted in Hall, *Puritans in the Balkans*, p. 167.

27. Quoted in Hall, *Puritans in the Balkans,* pp. 163-64.

28. Statement of House, March 21, in Rpt. No. 163, April 12, 1902; House to Peet, May 27 in Rpt. No. 202, Leishman to Hay, June 3, 1902, M46, Role 69.

29. Hall, *Puritans in the Balkans*, pp. 166-67.

30. Rpts. Nos. 134 and 145, February 6 and March 5, 1902, M46, Role 69.

31. Leishman to Tewfik, July 18, 1902 in Rpt. No. 233, Leishman to Hay, July 19, 1902, M46, Role 69.

32. Rpt. No. 155, Leishman to Hay, March 25, 1902, M46, Role 69.

33. Rpt. No. 163, Leishman to Hay, April 12, 1902, M46, Role 69.

34. Dispatch No. 423, Gueshov to Danev, March 5/18, 1902, TDIA, fund 176, opus 1, archive unit 1645, p. 94.

35. Biliotti to Lansdowne, March 12, 1902 in Bulgarian Academy of Science, Archives of the Institute of History, Collection IV, opus 136, archive unit 27, pp. 120-22; Letter No. 490, Dickinson to Leishman, February 25, 1902, T682.

36. Attached to Rpt. No. 134, Leishman to Hay, February 6, 1902, M46, Role 69.

37. Actually, $77,432.56 was contributed to the ransom fund by 2,261 people, in sums ranging from 10 cents to $5,000. In the archives of the American Farm School, a letter dated April 5, 1904, states that the remaining money is still in the hands of Kidder, Peabody and Co., and that "they are prepared to return it to subscribers." The letter goes on to say, however, that several large contributors have donated their subscriptions to American Board work in Bulgaria and Macedonia. People familiar with the history of the Farm School have suggested to me that these contributions enabled House to purchase the land and establish the Farm School in 1904. Letter, Frank H. Wiggins, Treasurer of the American Board to Irving W. Metcalf, Elyria, Ohio.

38. U.S. Congress, House. Committee on Claims, "Repayment of Ransom of Ellen Stone," (62nd Cong., 2nd sess., H. Rept. 807, May 31, 1912), pp. 2-3, 5.

39. I am indebted to Richard Cochran of the University of Notre Dame for the information and program notes on Katerina Tsilka's lecture tour of the United States.

BIBLIOGRAPHY

Primary Sources

Bulgaria. Ministry of Foreign Affairs. Tsentralen Dürzhaven Istoricheski Arkhivi, Fund 176, opus 1, archive units 1645, 1647, and 1762.

Bulgarian Academy of Sciences. Archives of the Institute of History. Collection IV, opus 92, archive units 74 and 80; opus 135, archive unit 21; and opus 136, archive unit 27.

Documents and Materials on the History of the Bulgarian People. Sofia: Bulgarian Academy of Science, Institute of History, 1969.

Goock, B.P. and Harold Temperley, eds. *The Near East. The Macedonian Problem and the Annexation of Bosnia, 1903-9. In British Documents on the Origins of the War, 1898-1914.* London: HMSO, 1953.

Great Britain. *Correspondence Respecting the Affairs of Southeastern Europe.* London: HMSO, 1903.

U.S. Congress. House. Committee on Claims. *Repayment of Ransom of Ellen Stone.* H. Rept. 807, 62nd Cong., 2nd sess., 31 May, 1912.

U.S. Department of State. Diplomatic Dispatches, Turkey. General Records of the Department of State, Record Group 59, National Archives Microfilm Publications. M46, Role 68 (1 May 1901 to 31 January, 1902); Role 69 (3 February to 26 June, 1902); and Role 70 (1 November, 1901 to 20 December, 1902).

—————————. Diplomatic Dispatches, Russia. General Records of the Department of State, Record Group 59, National Archives Microfilm Publications. M35, Role 58 (1 March to 31 October, 1901) and Role 59 (1 November, 1901 to 20 December, 1902).

—————————. Consular Dispatches, Constantinople. General Records of the Department of State, Record Group 59, National Archives Microfilm Publications, M77, Role 168 (23 December, 1896 to 5 June, 1902).

—————————. Diplomatic Instructions of the Department of State, Turkey. General Records of the Department of State. Record Group 59, National Archives Microfilm Publications, M77, Role 168 (23 December, 1896 to 5 June, 1902).

Secondary Sources

A. D. "35-godishnata ot Plenyavaneto na Misionerskata mis Ston." *Makedonski Vesti,* II, 70 (September, 1936), 1.

Anastasov, Iordan. *Yane Sandansky: Biografichen Ocherk.* Sofia: Izdatelstvo na Bülgarskata Komunisticheska Partiya, 1966.

Barton, James L. *The Missionary and His Critics.* New York: Fleming H. Revell, 1906.

Brailsford, N. H. *Macedonia, Its Races and Their Future.* London: Methuen and Co., 1906.

Bulgarian Academy of Sciences. *Istoriya na Bülgariya.* Sofia: Nauka i Izkustsvo, 1962, II.

Chernopeev, Peyu. *Dzhivot i deinost na Khristo Chernopeev.* Sofia: Central Party Archives, No. 2711.

Dakin, Douglas. *The Greek Struggle in Macedonia, 1897-1913.* Salonika: Institute for Balkan Studies, 1966.

Dobriyanov, Todor and Konstantin Pandev. "Dokumenti za Plenyavaneto na Amerikanskata Misionerka mis Ston." *Isvestiya na Dürzhavnite Arkhivi*, 33 (1977), pp. 99-133.

Hall, William Webster, Jr. *Puritans in the Balkans: The American Board Mission in Bulgaria, 1878-1918.* Sofia: Studia Historico-Philologica Serdicensia, Supplement, Vol. I, 1938.

Hamlin, Cyrus. *Among the Turks.* New York: Robert Carter and Brothers, 1877.

House, John H. "Facts with Reference to the Kidnapping, Captivity, and Ransoming of Miss Ellen M. Stone: Official Report." Salonika, Greece: American Farm School Archives, March 20, 1902.

Hurst, Michael, ed. *Key Treaties for the Great Powers, 1814-1914.* New York: St. Martin's Press, 1972, II.

"Iz Minaloto na Makedoniya." *Makedonski Vesti*, I, 16 and 17 (May, 1935).

Ivanov, Iordan, ed. *Süchineniya na Traiko Kitanchev.* Sofia: D. Golov, 1898.

Kharizanov, Ivan. "Aferata Mis Ston." *Den*, I, Nos. 26-37 (1945).

Khristov, Khristo. *Osvobozhdenieto na Bülgaria i Politika na Zapadnite Dürzhavi, 1876-1878.* Sofia: Nauka i Izkustvo, 1963.

Kiril, Patriarkh Bülgarski. *Bülgarskata Ekzarkhiya v Odrinskoto i Makedoniya cled Osvoboditelnata Voina, 1877-1878.* Sofia: Sinadalno Izdatelstvo, 1969, I.

Kresnensko-Razlozhkoto Vüstanie. *Dokladi ot Nauchnata Sesiya i Türzhestvenoto Chestvuvane na 90-godishnata ot Kresnensko-Raslozhkoto Vüstanie v Blagoevgrad.* Sofia: Bülgarskata Akademiya na Naukite, 1970.

Künchev, Vasil. *Pütuvane po dolinite na Struma, Mesta i Bregalnitsa.* In *Izbrani Proizvedeniya.* Ed. Khristo Khristov. Sofia: Nauka i Izkustvo, 1970, I.

Küosev, Dimo, ed. *Gotse Delchev: Pisma i Drugi Materiali.* Sofia: Bülgarskata Akademiya na Naukite, 1967.

Miletich, Liubomir, ed. *Materiali za Istoriyata na Makedonskoto Osvoboditelno Dvidzhenie.* Sofia: P. Glushkov, 1927 and 1928.
    Vol. V   *Spomeni na Damian Gruev, Boris Sarafov i Ivan Garvanov.*
    Vol. VI   *Solunskiyat Atentat.*
    Vol. VII *Dvizhenieto otsam Vardara i Borbata c Vürkhovistite.*
    Vol. VIII *Spomeni na Georcho Petrov.*
    Vol. IX *Pürviyat Tsentralen Komitet.*

Miller, William. *The Ottoman Empire and Its Successors, 1801-1927.* London: Cambridge University Press, 1927.

Monroe, Will S. *Bulgaria and Her People.* Boston: Page Co., 1914.

Moore, Frederick. *The Balkan Trail.* London: Smith, Elder and Co., 1906.

Nankivell, J. M. *A Life for the Balkans: The Story of John Henry House of the American Farm School.* New York: Fleming H. Revell, 1939.

Pandev, Konstantin, "L'Organisation Intérieure et le Comité Suprème, 1899-1901." *Études Historiques,* VI.

——————. "Nachalo na Makedono-Odrinskoto dvizhenie v Bülgariya, 1879--1894," *V Chest na Akademik Khristo A. Khristov.* Sofia: Bülgarskata Akademiya na Naukite, 1976, pp. 237-56.

——————. *Organizirano Natsionalnoosvoboditelno Dvizhenie v Makedoniya i Odrinsko, 1893-1903.* Diss. Institute of History, Bulgarian Academy of Sciences, 1970.

——————. "Politicheski Programi na Natsionalnoosvoboditelnoto Dvidzhenie v Makedoniya i Odrinkso do 1903g," *Pürviyat Kongres na Bülgarskoto Istorichesko Drudzhestvo.* Sofia: Institut za Istoriya, Vol. I, 1972, pp. 469-76.

——————. "Ustavi i Pravilnitsi na VMORO predi Ilindenskoto Preobrazhenskoto Vüstanie." *Izvestiya na Instituta za Istoriyata,* 21 (1970), 245-275.

Pears, Sir Edwin. *Forty Years in Constantinople.* London: Herbert Jenkins, 1916.

Poparsov, Peter. "Proizkhod na Revoliutsionnoto Dvizhenie v Makedoniya i Pürvite Stupki na Solunskiya 'Komitet' za Pridobivane Politicheski Prava na Makedoniya, Dadeni i ot Berlinskiya Dogovor." *Biuletin va Vremenoto Predstavitelstvo,* No. 8 (19 July, 1919).

Popov, Gerasim N. *Shestdeset Godini na Plenyavaneto na Elena Mis Ston, 1901-1961.* (Velingrad, Bulgaria, 25 August, 1961).

Riggs, Elias. *Reminiscences for My Children.* Constantinople: n.p., 1891.

Shaldev, Khristo. "Iz Zapiskite na Ivan Khadzhinikolov." *Iliustratsia Ilinden*, VI, No. 1 (1936), 1-15.

Shannon, R. T. *Gladstone and the Bulgarian Agitation, 1876.* London: Thomas Nelson and Sons, 1963.

Shopov, Peter. "Propagandnata i Prosvetnata Deinost na Amerikanskite bibleiski Obshtestva v Bulgarskite Zemi prez XIX vek." *Izvestiya na Instituta za Istoriya*, 23 (1974), pp. 149-184.

Siliyanov, Khristo. *Ilindenskoto Vüstanie.* Vol. I of *Osbovoditelni Borbi na Makedoniya.* Sofia: Dürzhavna Pechatnitsa, 1933.

Simeonov, Simeon. "Spomeni na P. G. Mandshukov za uchastieto mu v chetata na Gotse Delchev prez 1899g." *Izvestiya na: Dürzhavite Arkhivi*, 23 (1972), 175-202.

Simeonov, St. *Solunskoto Cüzaklyatie, 1898-1903.* Sofia: Nov Zhivot, 1921.

Sonnichsen, Albert. *Confessions of a Macedonian Bandit.* New York: Duffield and Co., 1909.

Stevenson, Francis Seymour, ed. *The Macedonian Question.* London: The Byron Society, 1902.

Stojanovic, Mihail D. *The Great Powers and the Balkans.* London: Cambridge University Press, 1939.

Stone, Ellen M. "Six Months Among Brigands." *McClure's Magazine*, XIX (May, June, July, September, and October, 1902), 2-14, 99-109, 222-232, 464-471; 562-570.

Stoyanov, Manüo. "Nachala na Protestantskata Propaganda v Bülgariya." *Izvestiya na Instituta za Istoriya*, 14-15 (1964), 45-67.

Stoyanov, Zakhari. *Zapiski po Bülgarskite Vüstaniya.* 1884: rpt. Sofia: Bulgarski Pisateli, 1977.

Strashimirov, Anton. *Krüstio Asenov.* Sofia: n.p., 1906.

Strong, William E. *The Story of the American Board.* Boston: Pilgrim Press, 1910.

Tsilka, Elena Katerina Stefanova. "Born Among Brigands." *McClure's Magazine*, XIX (August, 1902), 291-300.

Tomov, Lazar. *Spomeni na Revoliutsionnata Deinost v Serskiya Okrüg.* Sofia: Izdatelstvoto na Nationalniya Sevet na Otechestveniya Front, 1952.
————————. "Plenyanvaneto na mis El. Ston i g-zha Katerina Stefanova Tsilka." *Iliustratsia Ilinden*, V, No. 10 (1933), 25-30.

Washburn, George. *Fifty Years in Constantinople.* Boston: Houghton Mifflin and Co., 1909.

Yavorov, Peyu K. *Khaidutski Kopneniya* and *Gotse Delchev.* Vol. III of *Süchineniya.* 1909; rpt. Sofia: Bŭlgarski Pisateli, 1955.

INDEX

EAST EUROPEAN MONOGRAPHS

41. *Boleslaw Limanowski (1835-1935): A Study in Socialism and Nationalism.* By Kazimiera Janina Cottam. 1978.

42. *The Lingering Shadow of Nazism: The Austrian Independent Party Movement Since 1945.* By Max E. Riedlsperger. 1978.

43. *The Catholic Church, Dissent and Nationality in Soviet Lithuania.* By V. Stanley Vardys. 1978.

44. *The Development of Parliamentary Government in Serbia.* By Alex N. Dragnich. 1978.

45. *Divide and Conquer: German Efforts to Conclude a Separate Peace, 1914-1918.* By L. L. Farrar, Jr. 1978.

46. *The Prague Slav Congress of 1848.* By Lawrence D. Orton. 1978.

47. *The Nobility and the Making of the Hussite Revolution.* By John M. Klassen. 1978.

48. *The Cultural Limits of Revolutionary Politics: Change and Continuity in socialist Czecholslovakia.*

48. *The Cultural Limits of Revolutionary Politics: Change and Continuity in Socialist Czecholslovakia.* By David W. Paul. 1979.

49. *On the Border of War and Peace: Polish Intelligence and Diplomacy in 1937-1939 and the Origins of the Ultra Secret.* By Richard A. Woytak. 1979.

50. *Bear and Foxes: The International Relations of the East European States 1965-1969.* By Ronald Haly Linden. 1979.

51. *Czechoslovakia: The Heritage of Ages Past.* Edited by Ivan Volgye and Hans Brisch. 1979.

52. *Prime Minister Gyula Andrássy's Influence on Habsburg Foreign Policy.* By János Decsy. 1979.

53. *Citizens for the Fatherland: Education, Educators, and Pedagogical Ideals in Eighteenth Century Russia.* By J. L. Black. 1979.

54. *A History of the "Proletariat": The Emergence of Marxism in the Kingdom of Poland, 1870-1887.* By Norman M. Naimark. 1979.

55. *The Slovak Autonomy Movement, 1935-1939: A Study in Unrelenting Nationalism.* By Dorothea H. El Mallakh. 1979.

56. *Diplomat in Exile: Francis Pulszky's Political Activities in England, 1848-1840.* By Thomas Kabdebo. 1979.

57. *The German Struggle Against the Yugoslav Guerrillas in World War II: German Counter-Insurgency in Yugoslavia, 1941-1943.* By Paul N. Hehn. 1979.

58. *The Emergence of the Romanian National State.* By Gerald J. Bobango. 1979.

59. *Stewards of the Land: The American Farm School and Modern Greece.* By Brenda L. Marder. 1979.

60. *Roman Dmowski: Party, Tactics, Ideology, 1895-1907.* By Alvin M. Fountain II. 1980.

61. *International and Domestic Politics in Greece During the Crimean War.* By Jon V. Kofas. 1980.

62. *Fires on the Mountain: The Macedonian Revolutionary Movement and the Kidnapping of Ellen Stone.* By Laura Beth Sherman. 1980.